*The Kris Study Group of the
New York Psychoanalytic Institute*

Monograph I

The Kris Study Group of the
New York Psychoanalytic Institute

Monograph I

Beating Fantasies

Regressive Ego Phenomena
in Psychoanalysis

Edited by EDWARD D. JOSEPH, M.D.

INTERNATIONAL UNIVERSITIES PRESS, INC.
NEW YORK   NEW YORK

Manufactured in the United States of America

CONTENTS

Foreword

JACOB A. ARLOW, M.D.

DAVID BERES, M.D.

CHARLES BRENNER, M.D.

RUDOLPH M. LOEWENSTEIN, M.D.

THIS IS THE FIRST of a series of monographs which will report the activities of the Kris Study Group of the New York Psychoanalytic Institute. These reports will appear from time to time as the material and findings warrant. The over-all responsibility will rest with the members of the editorial board, who were greatly assisted in the preparation of the present volume by Dr. E. D. Joseph, its editor.

It seemed appropriate to the editorial board that the first publication of this series should contain the first panel section undertaken by the Kris Study Group. As coincidence had it, this first panel was the last of the meetings of the Study Group over which Ernst Kris presided. Following his death came the second panel presentation, one which had been planned prior to his death, but which was presented at the meetings directly afterward. The editors chose to present both panel reports which were planned under Kris's direction in one volume, and to include in this first monograph an appreciation of Ernst Kris and a history of study groups and their place in the development of psychoanalysis. Future publications in this series will be confined to reporting the work of the Study Group.

1

Ernst Kris, Teacher "How Much There Is to Learn"

BERNARD D. FINE, M.D.

I

IT IS DIFFICULT in a few paragraphs—or even several pages—to distill the essence of Ernst Kris, with his unusual talents and profound influence as a teacher. It is equally difficult to capture the many facets and subtle nuances that made his influence considerable.

To separate the legend from the man often presents further difficulties—but usually less so for those who have been in close and prolonged contact with the man and his work. We are fortunate at the New York Psychoanalytic Institute, and especially in the Kris Study Group, to have known him so well—to be aware how, in this instance, the legend is not far distant from the actual man.

Now, several years after his death, many of the things he stood for continue in his tradition—his Post-Graduate Study Group and the Gifted Adolescent Research Project, both at the New York

Prepared for presentation to the Kris Study Group, November 8, 1963.
Important contributions to this article have been made by personal contributions from Drs. Leon Altman, Stuart Asch, John McDevitt, and Oscar Sachs as well as by the reminiscences of other students and colleagues of Dr. Kris.

3

Psychoanalytic Institute, as well as the Child Study Center at Yale University Medical School.

Ernst Kris was born in Vienna on April 26, 1900, the younger son in a family where intellectual interests were valued highly, an attitude with which, we may assume, he identified early. His particular interest in art and culture as well as the search for and the organization of knowledge began in early adolescence. At this time he turned toward the study of art and its history while he was at bed rest for months because of an attack of rheumatic fever with carditis. He returned to the Gymnasium at the age of fourteen, but with the outbreak of war, the schools were closed during the winter months because of the fuel shortage. However, Kris used this time of enforced idleness to trespass into the University of Vienna's Department of Art History where Professor von Schlosser carried on seminar discussions with his students, who were few at this time because of military conscription. Kris's keen participation and precocious brilliance aroused the Professor's interest; however, Kris later caused the Professor some embarrassment when it became known that he had not yet reached matriculation age and was not even an undergraduate. Several years after formal matriculation, he obtained his Ph.D. in the history of art at the age of twenty-two, and soon afterward was appointed Curator of the Kunsthistorisches Museum in Vienna. There he earned distinction as a connoisseur of jewelry and as the author of a standard treatise on Renaissance intaglios and cameos. Prior to this publication he compiled, in collaboration with F. Cuchler, the museum's catalogue of its famous collection of cameos and intaglios, and because of this reputation, the Metropolitan Museum of Art in New York City invited him, in 1929, to catalogue its own collection of Post-Classical cameos.

While engaged in his work at the Kunsthistorisches Museum, a young medical student, Marianne Rie, first introduced Kris to Freud to advise him on his collection of cameos and intaglios. Kris later married Marianne Rie, who, as Marianne Kris, went on to become, in her own right, a child psychoanalyst and the leader of the Child Study Project at Yale.

Through his contacts with Freud, Kris "discovered" psychoanalysis and shortly afterward undertook a personal analysis at the Vienna Institute of Psychoanalysis. He soon became an enthusiastic and dedicated member of the small group of young analysts in the Vienna Psychoanalytic Society who worked in close personal contact with Freud. At that time, Kris was one of those who very quickly grasped the far-reaching importance of the new approach possible in psychoanalytic theory and practice with the introduction of structural concepts and ego psychology.

Starting in 1933, he published a series of papers on applied psychoanalysis which eventually appeared in book form in 1952, under the title *Psychoanalytic Explorations in Art*. Here Kris demonstrated his multiple talents. He combined professional scholarship as an art historian and a profound knowledge of psychoanalytic theory with personal perceptiveness, imagination, and originality. In 1933 he was asked by Freud to take over the editorship of *Imago* jointly with Robert Waelder. For the sake of this work, he renounced the study of medicine which he had started approximately six months earlier.

When Austria was taken over by Hitler in 1938, the Kris family followed Freud to England. During the war Kris served the British Broadcasting Corporation, analyzing Nazi radio broadcasts until he was sent to the United States by the British government, in July 1940, to contribute through this same work to the common war effort. Out of this work developed a book on German radio propaganda, published in collaboration with Hans Speier and others, which appeared in 1944. While still in England, one of his contributions (in "applied psychoanalysis") was the use of his professional skill and intuitive ability as a means of deriving vital specific and strategic information (objectively confirmed later) from enemy propaganda broadcasts.

In addition to the joint editorship of *Imago*, he was one of the editors of Freud's *Gesammelte Werke*. Together with Anna Freud and Marie Bonaparte, he edited Freud's letters to Wilhelm Fliess (*The Origins of Psychoanalysis*), and it was he who wrote the scholarly and illuminating introduction and notes for this volume. This work is generally considered to be a major contribution to historical research; Hoffer (1957) has commented that, had Ernst Kris contributed nothing else to psychoanalysis, his Introduction to *The Origins of Psychoanalysis* would have earned him our lasting admiration and thanks. He initiated the idea of a psychoanalytic periodical devoted to child psychology and psychoanalysis, and became one of the founders and managing editors of *The Psychoanalytic Study of the Child.* He also served on the Editorial Board of the *Journal of the American Psychoanalytic Association.*

In the last twelve years of his life his writings and interests became more exclusively oriented toward psychoanalytic theory, ego psychology, early childhood development, and the theory of psychoanalytic technique. In all of these fields, his work is generally regarded as among the most important and fundamental contributions to psychoanalysis since Freud.

To all who worked or studied with him, Ernst Kris was an unusual man with unusual talents. His friend, Professor E. H. Gombrich of London University, aptly described him in the *London Times* when he wrote: "Kris was among the very few in our time to approach the stature of a 'homo universalis.' " One of the most important of his talents was his special gift for teaching, which was the area in which I had most contact with him, both in his courses at the New York Psychoanalytic Institute and in the Kris Post-Graduate Study Group from the time of its inception. His particular talent as a good teacher seemed to come from his ability to be such a good student. Students felt that he was learning with them, even though he was elaborating on, clarifying, or suggesting some particular problem or formulation to the seminar. The feelings he imparted without any apparent conscious effort on his part were those of empathy with his students, of his willingness to learn, and of his devotion to his work. A quotation from Albert Einstein is also quite appropriate to these remarks about Kris as a teacher: "It is the supreme art of the teacher to awaken joy in the creative expression and knowledge." I believe Ernst Kris achieved that goal.

Above all else, Ernst Kris had the ability to "stimulate" his students. What he taught his students was important, but much more important was the way in which he stimulated an exciting urge to ask questions and to search for answers. Much of this came from his early experiences in learning and searching on his own—a sublimation which he never relinquished.

Among those whose lives are devoted to intellectual work, there is usually one certain teacher who stands out, one who is able to transmit his enthusiasm and pleasure in teaching and in inviting others to participate in the world of ideas which is so important to him. Kris was such a teacher, and we experienced what he experienced—a great pleasure in thought and knowledge. But more than this—there was a palpable and sincere interest in the class or group or seminar, a love of, and pleasure in, teaching as well as the intense desire to have everyone participate in his zeal and enthusiasm. Once the spark within was ignited by him, it became a mutually and highly satisfying experience. One colleague who described several analytic supervisory sessions recalled how Kris "listened ardently and spoke ardently." He also recalled two particular incidents of his many control sessions: "Once I must have been talking to him about my patient in a dry, detached, coldly clinical or even disinterested manner" when Dr. Kris remarked, "I would like to be able to take the temperature in your office— you know, feel the emotional climate in which you and your patient operate." Also, when another patient was presented who had become hostile, negative, and had regressed to primitive, narcissistic, "stupid" states, Kris suggested that the analyst offer the helpful interpretation to the patient that, "You know you hold yourself very far away from me." His feeling about the need for close contact, continuing interest, and tact was always outstanding and appropriate.

He wanted to teach curiosity and particularly how to think. A seminar with Kris was not, and could not be, a passive experience. "How much there is to learn" was a remark he frequently used, which was part of his teaching and of his way of life. He also used a borrowed phrase and pressed it home repeatedly,"Look for the lilacs in January"—a search for which he had the greatest facility himself.

One cannot actually separate his personal qualities from those he used so remarkably in his work and teaching. Perhaps the most outstanding were his enthusiasm for knowledge, his own encyclopedic knowledge, his genuine love of teaching, and his great charm—compounded of tact, respect, and genuine interest. The full range of his activities is striking—from psychoanalysis itself, through art and other creative processes, teaching and specific research projects, into one of his latest interests, horticulture, and the cultivation of his own garden at home.

A striking, but not unusual example of how Kris worked as moderator and teacher came in a meeting (February 13, 1957) of the Post-Graduate Study Group which he attended shortly before his death. To quote from Charles Brenner's excellent summary of the meeting which was a panel discussion on Beating Fantasies

> In general, the evening's discussion centered about the relation between beating fantasies and specific events of the patient's childhood. . . . In the course of discussion, Dr. Kris made a suggestion which seemed to the Chairman to be a particularly illuminating one and to permit for the first time a clear understanding of the reasons for the great variations in the symptomatology and character structures of persons with beating fantasies as well as of the relationships among these variations. Dr. Kris proposed that the infantile wish to be loved sexually by the father was often (perhaps regularly) conceived by the child as being beaten by him. Presumably this would correspond to an equally frequent infantile sexual theory: that, what the father does to his sexual partner (i.e., mother) is to beat her. Dr. Kris pointed to the importance of anal as well as of sadomasochistic experiences and impulses in the genesis of such an idea in the mind of the child. If this suggestion is correct, Dr. Kris pointed out, the question about beating fantasies in clinical practice would no longer be why they are there. That question would rather be why beating fantasies had assumed and maintained such importance in the psychosexual life of a particular patient.

In his characteristic way, Kris had abstracted, reformulated, and synthesized much of the preceding theoretical and clinical discussion into an original and provocative generalization.

In one of his most recent papers, "On Some Vicissitudes of Insight in Psychoanalysis" Kris, (1956) described the integrative function of the ego as shown in the "good analytic hour." He states that such "good hours" gradually come into their own after some memory or experience has presented itself—or after dreams and associations and memories begin to flow—"at times new elements are introduced as if they had always been familiar so well do they seem to fit . . . and often shortly after when the analyst interprets, all he needs to say can be put into a question. The patient may well do the summing up by himself, and he himself arrive at conclusions. Such hours, naturally not all as smooth or complete, seem as if prepared in advance ... here the integrative functions of the ego are at work ... many a time we can watch the progressive establishment of this state of mind, when what was at first 'intellectual,' 'flat,' and 'two-dimensional' becomes 'real,' 'concrete,' and 'three-dimensional.' "

While the intent and meaning of Kris's paper is specifically related to individual psychoanalytic theory and technique, nevertheless the description of the process gives, quite eloquently, the feeling of what so often went on in a "teaching hour" between Kris and the group. There would often be the initial hesitant steps, even the resistance to any opening comments and speculations, then he would question or comment briefly himself, and the material would come slowly and with many facets. Then followed a reorganization of thoughts and material, guided by another interpolation from Kris, and the entire group would begin to contribute and understand along a "final common pathway." Often a question or "clarification" from Kris would be enough, and again a subject that was "intellectual and flat became real and three-dimensional." What the relationship of this group phenomenon is to the analytic interaction and the teaching process cannot be elaborated on here. However, it does give the flavor and an accurate picture of what occurred in many seminar experiences with Kris.

In closing I cite Hartmann's (1957) eloquent tribute: "Ernst Kris was a man of wide and genuine interests far beyond the limits of his chosen field. In his contacts with people, he was intensely alive, brilliantly imaginative and intuitive, and responded with rare subtlety and understanding to individual nuances in the people he met.... He was an extremely complex human being, and even after many years of close contact with him, one could still be surprised by a new and admirable finesse or elegance of his feeling or thought." Most of these attributes had to do with Kris as a person and were a part of him at all times, not only when he was before a seminar. Yet they were essential in making him the great teacher that he was. It was his innate sense of tact and decency, his charm and warmth, his fairness and honesty, his

sincere and real interest in his students, and finally his inde-
fatigable energy and enthusiasm for teaching which will make
forever contagious his credo, "how much there is to learn."

BIBLIOGRAPHY

Hartmann, H. (1957), Ernst Kris (1900-1957). *The Psychoanalytic Study of the Child,*
    12:9-15. New York: International Universities Press.
Hoffer, W. (1957), Obituary, Ernst Kris (1900-1957). *Int. J. Psychoanal.,* 38:359-
    362.
Kris, E. (1956), On Some Vicissitudes of Insight in Psychoanalysis. *Int. J. Psy-
    choanal.,* 37:445-455.
Loewenstein, R. M. (1957), In Memoriam, Ernst Kris 1900-1957. *J. Amer. Psychoanal.
    Assn.,* 5:741-743.
Ritvo, S. (1957), Ernst Kris. *Psychoanal. Quart.,* 26:248-250.

The Ernst Kris Study Group Continuing a Psychoanalytic Tradition

BURNESS E. MOORE, M.D.

IN THE PAST DECADE the Ernst Kris Study Group has become a significant influence on psychoanalysis in America. The inspiration provided by the group and the example of its organization have contributed to a major advance in psychoanalytic education—the continuation of systematic study into the postgraduate period. This development is a logical extension of a similar forward step inaugurated on an undergraduate level by the establishment of the first psychoanalytic training institute in Berlin in 1920. Recognition of the intellectual ferment stimulated by the activities of the Kris Group led to the consideration in this paper of study groups as an analytic phenomenon. From this historical perspective the beginning and evolution of the Ernst Kris Study Group will be described as a preliminary to a later examination of the psychology of this specific group.

Study and discussion groups are a tradition in psychoanalysis, and the vital role they have played in its development is clearly evident in the history of the movement. The precursor of the analytic study group was Freud's association with friends on social occasions, during walks and on vacation trips, when similar scientific interests led to an exchange of clinical experiences and ideas. Such personal contacts with Breuer over a number of years

11

resulted in a fruitful scientific collaboration until their estrangement. Afterward, Fliess filled the intellectual gap and for a time was Freud's only audience for his exposition of the development of psychoanalysis.[1] Slowly, however, Freud's theories gained adherents; he had more than one sympathetic listener. The banding together of devoted pupils and colleagues was inevitable in an unfriendly medical world and resulted in a wholesome cross-fertilization of brilliant minds. For the younger men who were attracted to psychoanalysis, contact with older colleagues constituted a preceptorship by which the clinical wisdom of their elders was passed on to the new generation. Gradually, of course, such preceptorships gave way to more formal training in the form of lectures, seminars, and didactic and supervised analyses. Even the organized training was, however, the outgrowth of informal discussion groups, and the tradition of such associations has been continued through the years, to the great enrichment of psychoanalytic theory and technique.

Both Freud (1914) and Jones (1955), as his biographer, have given us accounts of the beginning of the first psychoanalytic study group. In the autumn of 1902 Freud, apparently at the suggestion of Stekel, invited Adler, Kahane, Reitler and Stekel to meet for discussion of his work at his residence. These meetings, which took

[1] In his introduction to *The Origins of Psychoanalysis* (Freud, 1887-1902), Kris calls attention to the extent to which Fliess served as a sounding board for Freud's formulations in the friendly and encouraging exchange of letters between them: "In the early years of their correspondence Freud kept Fliess informed of his work in progress and sent him copies of everything he wrote. Fliess soon became the confidant to whom he communicated clinical material, his latest findings, and the first formulations of new theories. Thus we find among Freud's letters, not only half-thought-out outlines of new ideas and plans for future research, but some finished essays that were scarcely to be surpassed in his later works" (p. 13). The dynamic meaning of this relationship has been analyzed in specific terms by Edith Buxbaum (1951): *The Interpretation of Dreams* had for Freud a subjective meaning in that it was a piece of his self-analysis, concerned with his reaction to the death of his father. In Fliess, Freud found a transference figure on whom he could project his thoughts and emotions and thereby work through his oedipal complex. Without such an intense personal relationship at this time, the creative process represented in Freud's remarkable self-analysis may not have been possible in the form in which it was expressed. However, while aiding creativity, the involvement between two people may also lead to distortion of objectivity in the exercise of critical evaluation and judgment. Interesting questions are raised as to the effect on creativity and objectivity of the diffusion of libidinal and aggressive feelings among several individuals within a group.

place about the oblong table in Freud's waiting-room, were for the express "intention of learning, practising and spreading the knowledge of psycho-analysis" (Freud, 1914, p. 25). Later, others joined the circle, often only temporarily, but some found a permanent place in the history of psychoanalysis. These included Federn, Hitschmann, Rank, Sadger, Ferenczi, Tausk, Jekels,, Hans Sachs, and Silberer. To this group, as visitors, also came Eitingon, Jung, Binswanger, Abraham, Brill, Jones and many others. At first Stekel reported the discussions in the Sunday edition of the *Neues Wiener Tagblatt,* but after Otto Rank joined in 1906, "the little society acquired in him a zealous and reliable secretary" (Freud, 1914, p. 25). From these "Psychological Wednesday Evenings," as they were called, the first psychoanalytic society came into being in 1908.[2]

It is safe to assume that most, if not all, psychoanalytic societies had their inception in similar discussion and study groups.[3] That the New York Psychoanalytic Society had such an origin is indicated by Brill (1938) and Oberndorf (1927). Jones (1955) mentions already existing psychoanalytic groups which enrolled themselves as Branch Societies of the International Association after the Nuremburg Congress in 1910. The first of these was the group from Berlin, which grew up about Abraham and Eitingon. Even the International Association itself owed its beginning to the forma-

---

[2] In the Eleventh A. A. Brill Memorial Lecture, Herman Nunberg (1959) presented excerpts from *The Minutes of the Vienna Psychoanalytic Society* (Nunberg and Federn, 1962), as recorded by Rank from 1906 to 1915. These provide fascinating insights with regard to the personalities, the conflicts, and the working together of the members of this earliest psychoanalytic enclave. Its composition was heterogeneous, consisting of educators and writers as well as physicians. Since its aim was the discussion of psychological problems, papers were read and books reviewed, but in the informal atmosphere of a small and intimate group, personal problems and even confessions were also discussed. It is understandable that along with mutual stimulation there was much ambivalence and friction. Through it all, Freud was the disciplined leader, patient and tolerant, though he could be caustic too when there was need. The serious intent of its members was indicated by the regularity and frequency of the meetings, the discussion of subjects according to certain rules, and the faithful (though sometimes too abbreviated) reporting of discussions by a secretary.

[3] As Bertram D. Lewin (1959) points out, such study groups were also the nuclei around which institutes were later established. Until about 1950 the term "Study Group" was used by the American Psychoanalytic Association to designate what is now called "Training Center." Historically, therefore, the study group has been both proto society and proto institute.

tion of a "Psychoanalytic Circle" or little "Freud Group" at the Burghölzli psychiatric clinic in Zurich. Freud's enthusiasm at the first recognition of his work abroad and the close ties he established with the Zurich group led to Jung's organization, at Jones's suggestion, of a general gathering of those interested in Freud's work at Salzburg in 1908. This "Meeting for Freudian Psychology," as Jung designated it, was the first of the International Psycho-analytical Congresses.

In the early years of psychoanalysis there was an eagerness on the part of his followers to spread knowledge of Freud's work and to gain for it some recognition. One way by which these objectives could be attained was the formation of groups of interested persons for discussion. Thus Ernest Jones (1955) comments on Freud's lectures[4] at Clark University: "New England was by no means unprepared to listen to Freud's new doctrines. In the autumn of 1908 . . . I had held two or three colloquiums at which sixteen people were present."[5] Where the atmosphere was favorable, these groups formed the nuclei for new psychoanalytic societies which were organized along conventional lines. The societies were the spearheads for the new movement. They provided a common meeting ground as well as a unity of purpose and action and gave to each member the strength and prestige of a group at least outwardly devoted to the same goals.

Dissemination of Freud's ideas and the advancement of the movement was thus one impelling motivation in the formation of

[4] Helene Deutsch (1940) quotes Freud's comments regarding his lecture tour in America: "It was like the realization of an incredible daydream when I stepped up to the lecturer's chair in Worcester to give my first lectures on psychoanalysis. So then! Psychoanalysis was no longer a phantasm; it had become a valuable piece of reality." She adds, "One notes here, in his indirect likening of it to illusion, Freud's rejection of isolation and the strong need he felt to give his ideas the full value of reality through their recognition and acceptance by the world at large. It was out of this need that the psychoanalytic group had to come into being."

[5] It is probable that Jones was referring to meetings in the home of Morton Prince. Beginning in 1906, these were attended, every month or so for several years, by most of the Boston contributors to the *Journal of Abnormal Psychology*. The Harvard neurologist, James J. Putnam, seems to have been more interested in psychoanalysis than his colleagues after Freud's lectures at Clark University. Until his death in 1918, he met occasionally with Isador Coriat and L. E. Emerson, a philosopher, to discuss the philosophical and ethical implications of psychoanalysis (Oberndorf, 1953). It was not until ten years later that the Boston Psychoanalytic Institute was founded (see Hendrick, 1961).

psychoanalytic groups. What Nunberg said of the men who formed the Wednesday Evening Group[6] was true in general of many of the analytic pioneers. They were "a group of men in search of new ideas and of a leader, and on the other hand Freud was a lonely man who had made important discoveries and wished to share them with others" (Nunberg, 1962). But there was an intellectual as well as an emotional basis for their gatherings. In this intelligent, gifted group there was an awareness of the limitations of knowledge with regard to the workings of the human mind and an acute dissatisfaction with the status of that knowledge. The exchange of ideas and experiences possible in small groups provided an opportunity to add to the existing knowledge to be gained individually in the new field. In discussing the Second International Psycho-analytical Congress in Nuremburg in 1910, Jones (1955) mentions having written to Freud beforehand to suggest that a collective study of symbolism be instituted. Though a committee was actually formed for this purpose, little came of it.[7]

It was perhaps too much to expect such an effort to be effective in a new and as yet poorly integrated body. Moreover, the objectives of collective study and investigation are somewhat inconsistent with the function of societies. The latter bind together the adherents of psychoanalysis, give them official representation, and provide a forum for the formal presentation and discussion of the results of study. Whereas the early societies—and many today as well—were small enough to permit general and informal

[6] "We have learned from our analyses that in order to heal inner conflicts it is necessary first to bare their sources and thus to understand them. We have also learned that we often project our own conflicts onto the external world. It seems safe to assume that the urge of these men to understand and to heal their fellow men reflected to a great extent their own need for help. . . . And, indeed, at the meetings of the Society they discussed not only the problems of others, but also their own difficulties. . . . It is true that they seem to have been neurotics, but no more so than many others who are not considered ill" (Nunberg, 1962, p. xx). Though devoted to the psychology of the individual these early psychoanalytic meetings were therefore the first group therapy sessions.

[7] This early suggestion for a collective clinical and theoretical study of psychoanalytic subjects is now being followed in the activities of the Ernst Kris Study Group. The very subject mentioned by Jones, symbolism, was selected by one of its Sections in 1959-1960, and members of the Group subsequently participated in a panel discussion at the meeting of the American Psychoanalytic Association in May, 1960.

discussion and so continue the opportunities for a fruitful exchange of ideas, the size of the membership often became too large for these objectives to be achieved within the conventional framework. Divergent viewpoints and personality clashes, as well as important theoretical differences, frequently interfered with effective co-operation. These limitations resulted in a continuation of the smaller groups reminiscent of Freud's earlier years. There was then—as there continues to be now—the association of a few friends with similar ideals, who were emotionally compatible and could work together co-operatively. Although their influence upon each other has been tremendous, they were in a sense simply studying together, and no particular recognition was taken of the effect of their mutual effort. For this reason, the history of these relationships and of their activities is necessarily sketchy. Only a few of the many will be mentioned.

After the operations for cancer made it difficult for Freud to speak in public, he no longer attended society meetings. Instead, for a time during the 1920's, *erweiterte Vorstands Sitzungen* took place in his home. These constituted enlarged meetings of the Board of the Vienna Psychoanalytic Society since, in addition to the officers, there were some regular and some occasional participants from among the membership, numbering at maximum about twenty people. Called at irregular intervals, these gatherings were mostly for the purpose of securing Freud's opinion on various issues of interest to psychoanalysis. In the following decade Freud's regular contacts with a group were restricted to an even more limited circle which included Edward Bibring, Paul Federn, Anna Freud, Heinz Hartmann, Willi Hoffer, Ernst Kris, Richard Sterba, and Robert Waelder.[8]

In addition to the small group gathered about Freud, many analysts whose names are now associated with significant contributions to the literature had already started independent study. In

[8] I am indebted to Dr. Heinz Hartmann and Mr. Ernst Federn for information about the members of Freud's circle, and to Mrs. Berta Bornstein, Dr. Edith Jacobson, and Dr. Marianne Kris for accounts of the Berlin and Vienna *Kinderseminaren*. Dr. Richard Karpe has kindly provided the history of the Prague group. The author is entirely responsible for the synthesis of their reminiscences, which cannot be verified readily by access to historical sources. Apologies are therefore due to any persons whose names may have been omitted.

this trend Fenichel, recognized early as a brilliant and gifted young man, was a leading spirit. In Vienna, as early as 1919, he invited a few medical students, among them Edward and Grete Bibring and Wilhelm Reich, to join him in the study of psychoanalysis. When he moved to Berlin, he initiated a similar group there. Rudolph Loewenstein was a member until 1923, when he left for Paris just as Edith Jacobson joined the small circle. At this time the members were only four or five in number, but by 1926 the association of friends had turned into a recognized study group, and by 1929 about twenty persons were active. The *Kinderseminar,*[9] so called because of the comparative youth of its members, was entirely independent of the Berlin Training Institute and provided a forum in which the younger analysts could thrash out their own ideas. Meetings took place at the homes of various members and were alternately devoted to clinical and theoretical subjects. "Papers were given when one had something to say; a clinical case would be presented when one had a problem" (Bornstein, 1959). Fenichel remained the leading figure in the group although Schultz-Henke presided at a few meetings and Wilhelm Reich participated again in the last years of the seminar.

About 1933 the rise of the Hitler regime started a general exodus of psychoanalysts from Berlin. A recent analytic student from Berlin, Emanuel Windholz, was already established in Prague and, with others sympathetic to psychoanalysis, gave assistance to several refugees. Frances Deri was on a trip to Prague in 1933 to address this small group, which included Richard Karpe, then a young pediatrician, and Marietta Karpe, when she heard about the *Reichstagsbrand* and the arrest of a relative. She decided to settle in Prague and became the leader of the Prague Study Group, supported by, but independent of, the Vienna Institute. Henry Lowenfeld, Annie Reich, Steff Bornstein, Christina Olden and Liselotte Gerö strengthened the little band in 1933 and 1934, and Edward Kronold and Edith Jacobson came a little later. When

---

[9] A partial list of the members of the Berlin *Kinderseminar* includes: Gustav Bally, Berta Bornstein, Steff Bornstein, Frances Deri, Otto Fenichel, Robert Fliess, Erich Fromm, George Gerö, Alfred Gross, Erich Haas, Edith Jacobson, Eric Kraft, Marianne Kris, Barbara Lantos, Henry Lowenfeld, Annie Reich, Wilhelm Reich and Harold Schultz-Henke.

Frances Deri moved to Los Angeles in 1936 at the invitation of Ernst Simmel, Fenichel replaced her as the leader of the group. Analytic activities were increased after his arrival and included even Sunday picnics. For a long time, Steff Bornstein conducted a very stimulating child study group which attracted analysts, candidates, nursery school teachers and just plain parents. Of the participants in this group, Yela Lowenfeld and Michalina Fabian became analysts after their immigration to the United States. The group in Prague never became the nucleus of a training institute because all except three of the analysts left Prague before March, 1939 (Karpe, 1960).

Meanwhile, the efforts of Anna Freud to develop the new field of child analysis led to the formation of another important study group. While she was staying with Freud at the Tegel Sanitarium near Berlin in 1928, when Freud was being fitted with a new prosthesis, Anna Freud was asked by some of the Berlin group to conduct some seminars on child analysis. These were continued in Vienna, and by 1931 there was a considerable group[10] which met regularly for the purpose of considering the technical problems posed in the psychoanalytic treatment of children. Although its name described its subject matter rather than its participants, this group too was called the *Kinderseminar*. By 1936 nearly thirty people were participating, and it was decided to divide the seminar into small "colloquia," which were to deal with special subjects. This was an organizational procedure which originated with the Berlin Institute after clinical seminars had become too large. However, the large seminar was retained in addition to the colloquia groups. The same plan was followed in Vienna, the larger group becoming a technical seminar which dealt with both adults and children. In the reorganization of the Ernst Kris Study Group, the pattern was repeated again.

Thus the development and growth of psychoanalytic study

---

[10] "The Vienna *Kinderseminar* was at first limited solely to practicing child analysts. The original members were, as far as I know, Anny Angel, Marianne Kris, Edith Buxbaum, and Edith Sterba. I entered this group in 1931, when I went to Vienna. Only in the later 1930's were analysts who did not practice child analysis admitted to the meetings of the *Kinderseminar*. They were Grete and Edward Bibring, Kurt and Ruth Eissler, Heinz Hartmann, Richard Sterba, René Spitz, and a few more whom I do not remember" (Bornstein, 1959).

groups has been much the same despite variations.[11] Such associations provide a medium for the sharing of clinical experiences, the development of theory, and the introduction and testing of technical innovations. In an atmosphere of intense reciprocal interest, ideas are freely exchanged, subsequently developed individually or jointly, and then rediscussed and modified. In view of the mutual stimulation, interaction, and joint elaboration of ideas, it is surprising that individuality has been maintained so consistently. In the final elaboration, perhaps narcissism exacts its tribute. Usually such associations have not given rise to collaborative papers, though there are a few exceptions. An important one has been the work of Hartmann, Kris, and Loewenstein,[12] whose joint publications have contributed vastly to ego psychology and general psychoanalytic theory.

Whether designated as study groups or not, the regular meeting of friends for scientific pursuits has contributed greatly to psychoanalysis in the past, and the organization and promotion of such gatherings is important for its further progress.[13] Training and

[11] A large, organized study group which preceded the Kris Study Group is worthy of mention. In 1947, Paul Federn began a weekly Freud Seminar in his home for a group of social workers. After his death in 1950, the members of the Seminar decided to continue as the Paul Federn Study Group. Though there were a few medical analysts and psychiatrists in the original group, the membership now consists almost entirely of nonmedical professionals in the behavioral sciences. The program has been limited to the study of Freud and contemporary analysts of the Freudian school. Monthly meetings were led by Robert Waelder from 1951-1953, by Robert Bak from 1953 to 1955, by Mark Kanzer in 1954, and by Mortimer Ostow from 1956 to 1958. In 1959 Richard Sterba led a seminar on Freud's case history of an infantile neurosis (Federn, 1960).

[12] There is no indication that the three thought of their activities as those of a study group. They were simply colleagues working together on certain common interests. In this, their motives were similar to those of Freud and Breuer. In contrast, more recent associations of this nature have explicitly acknowledged the objectives of study and discussion out of which common interests may emerge. A case in point is the study group formed by Jacob Arlow, David Beres, Charles Brenner, and Martin Wangh, which has continued uninterrupted over fifteen years. That these associations were of the same nature is indicated by their linkage in conversation within the New York Psychoanalytic Society. The older associates were jocularly referred to as the "Big Three"; the younger colleagues as the "Little Four." Their recognition of the values to be derived from co-operative effort is evident in the contributions in leadership which both groups have made to the Ernst Kris Study Group.

[13] Movement in this direction is already well advanced (see Lewin and Ross, 1960, pp. 337-340). The trend is toward Institute sponsorship and organization of small groups for postgraduate study and training along the lines of the Ernst Kris Study Group. A Committee on Post-Graduate Development has been es-

investigation will profit from such contacts, for the limited clinical experience possible with modern technique makes it desirable to pool experience. However, many problems are associated with the attempt to foster groups.[14] Usually such associations are spontaneous and voluntary. If they are created by *diktat*, they dissolve when the authority is weakened or removed. The degree of organization may be an advantage or a handicap. In a friendly and informal atmosphere new and untried thoughts can be expressed freely, expanded by the experience and theories of others, and perfected later. However, if the organization is too loose and discussion too casual, many promising ideas may be lost because they are unrecorded, their significance not recognized at the time, and the leads not systematically pursued. A study of the gradual evolvement of a modern study group may contribute to the methodology of psychoanalytic training and investigation and to group problem solving—not that any such group should be accepted as an inflexible model. Groups vary with the characters and temperaments of members, and there is naturally an ever changing quality about them. Even within a single group there is an unending evolution. Nevertheless, as Freud (1921) has demonstrated, the study of the group itself can be instructive.

The Ernst Kris Study Group

What is now known as the Ernst Kris Study Group began, like its predecessors, out of the desire of students to learn psychoanalytic principles and technique. However, unlike the earlier groups,

---

tablished for this purpose by the American Psychoanalytic Association under the Chairmanship of Dr. Leo Rangell.

[14] Not the least of such problems involves the matter of time and distance. This point is illustrated by the experience of the American Psychoanalytic Association. The panel discussions which are a popular feature of its present-day programs were the outgrowth of an attempt to develop national study groups. Members who were interested in the same problems were invited to meet as committees during the semi-annual meetings. Conflicting demands for time and space made it necessary that such meetings be scheduled by the Program Committee, and gradually they took on their present form. Small discussion groups, reinstated in the programs of the Association two years ago, have elicited enthusiastic participation. Despite the sacrifice of time and the travel required, adequate organization makes possible a high level of productivity from study groups with a national membership, as demonstrated by the experience of the Group for the Advancement of Psychiatry.

which were the *anlagen* of societies or functioned independently, the Ernst Kris Study Group originated from the teaching activities of an institute and developed with the aid and under the sponsorship of an institute and its corresponding society.[15]

For many years Ernst Kris had taught courses in ego psychology and the technique of psychoanalysis to third-year students of the New York Psychoanalytic Institute. In the Spring of 1953 the members of his class[16] discussed with him their desire to form a study group, as several other classes had done, and asked that he be their leader. In reviewing his third-year courses, Kris felt that an adequate survey of ego psychology had not been possible and that he had made a selection of certain problems related to clinical interests. Now there was a well-integrated group of students, eager and ready to learn more because of their experience with patients. With his usual enthusiasm, Kris was willing to undertake this new project, but he wanted to integrate the study group within the framework of the Institute curriculum.[17] After consultation with the Curriculum and Educational Committees it was decided to offer the study group as an elective fourth-year course which would meet once a month. The prospectus of the course provides a succinct outline of the plan of the study group: "Individual papers and groups of publications on psychoanalytic theory will be discussed and special emphasis will be placed on the relation to clinical problems. The topics for discussion will be selected by the participants and guest speakers will be invited."[18]

The first meeting of each year was devoted to planning the program of subjects to be discussed. What could have been a dull task

[15] Seminars given by Heinz Hartmann, Ernst Kris, and Lawrence Kubie had provided the stimulus for an earlier study group organized by Leo Spiegel. Acting out and technical procedures for dealing with resistances arising out of religion were among the topics discussed under the leadership of Edith Jacobson, Lawrence Kubie, and others. Though the continuation of the group as a part of the New York Psychoanalytic Institute curriculum was discussed, it was not possible at that time (Spiegel, 1963).

[16] Nine students were in this class: Frank Berchenko, Benedict J. Bernstein, Kenneth T. Calder, Bernard D. Fine, Avraam T. Kazan, Leo S. Loomie, Jr., Howard N. Scal, Howard H. Schlossman, and Herbert Weider. However, before the first meeting of the study group, those registered had increased to fifteen, and during the first year twenty-one persons attended.

[17] From notes taken at a meeting of the Curriculum Committee of the New York Psychoanalytic Institute, May 13, 1953.

[18] From the *Catalogue of the New York Psychoanalytic Institute* (1953-1954).

was never that under the direction of Ernst Kris. His inspiration
and broad knowledge of psychoanalysis made it a fascinating survey of those subjects vital to psychoanalysis and most in need of
clarification. The list of subjects covered in the first three years re-
veals the breadth of interest of the group and the energy with
which it pursued an ever-deepening comprehension of psychoanalysis. Though the original plan had been to discuss a different
topic each month, it was always difficult to be satisfied with a single
discussion period, and frequently two or even three sessions were
devoted to different aspects of the same subject.

The conduct of the meetings demonstrated Kris's unusual syn-
thesizing function which, among other qualities, contributed to
his remarkable leadership. In a brief introduction, he would re-
capitulate the reasons for the selection of a subject and ask for
questions from the group. After collecting a sufficient number,
Kris would repeat the questions, grouping them in the process,
finding connections and correlations, and rephrasing them in
terms which reflected their theoretical and technical implications
and their relevancy to the immediate problem at hand as well as
to the framework of psychoanalytic theory. Having sketched in
broad terms the lines which the discussion should follow, he would
turn the meeting over to the guest, but he always felt free to
interrupt, to pose another question, or to add some clarification of
his own. Students were encouraged to follow this example, and by
reformulating their sometimes halting questions, Kris helped to
elicit the maximum of information from a guest.[19]

During the first three years of the study group this plan was followed without significant deviation. There was, however, a massive growth in membership and enthusiasm for the activities of
the group. In the beginning Kris had anticipated that the study
group would be composed of students of the Institute during their
fourth year only, and that there would be a turnover of member-

[19] This trait is reminiscent of Freud. Writing of Jung's first visit to Freud,
Jones (1955, p. 32) relates Jung's own account of the interview. Jung had much
to tell and ask and talked with intense animation for three hours. "Then the
patient, absorbed listener interrupted him with the suggestion that they conduct
their discussion more systematically. To Jung's great astonishment Freud proceeded to
group the contents of the harangue under several precise headings that enabled
them to spend the further hours in a more profitable give and take."

ship each year. However, so great was the interest, that relatively few students dropped out after their fourth year or even after their graduation from the Institute. Of the twenty-one who attended during the first year, eighteen were still active after six years; two had moved, and one was a special student. The attendance was augmented each year by almost the entire membership of each fourth-year class and even by a few of the older members of the New York Psychoanalytic Society. In the first four years the attendance increased from twenty-one to thirty, to forty-six, and to sixty-three. The registrants in 1962 numbered over one hundred.

By the spring of 1956 the very size of the group began to hamper its effectiveness. Although meetings were still held around a big oval table in the Board Room of the New York Psychoanalytic Institute, the participants were three and four rows deep. Kris adamantly refused to meet in an auditorium since he felt that the change would interfere with the free give-and-take of informal discussion. As it was, too few members had an opportunity to participate except by listening. Therefore, at its first meeting in the Fall of 1956, he asked the group to consider possible revisions in the arrangements and procedures to be followed at the meetings. In particular, he hoped that some format might be devised by which relevant clinical material could be presented to the group to illustrate some of the concepts which were being studied. Although the earlier type of meeting continued through the fall, it was decided to devote several Winter and Spring meetings to discussion of beating fantasies and regressive ego phenomena according to a new procedure. Volunteers were asked to prepare case histories of patients demonstrating these phenomena. These were mimeographed and distributed well in advance of the meetings. Drs. Jacob A. Arlow and Charles Brenner were invited to direct and co-ordinate the activities of the two subgroups participating in the study of these topics. This work was carried out in separate meetings, and the result was a panel of prepared discussants who introduced the subject to the entire Study Group and sought to answer the questions directed to them.

The meetings of January 14th and February 11th, 1957, were devoted to beating fantasies. There was universal enthusiasm for

the new form which the meetings had taken. Kris was pleased and
felt that the problem of meeting the needs of the expanding organization had been at least partially solved. He looked upon the
study group as an important instrument of postgraduate study,
training, and investigation. Through it he hoped that the opportunity could be provided for the continuing growth and development of those who would some day have to take over the responsibility for psychoanalytic teaching.

Ernst Kris died on February 27, 1957. He had, among his many
other accomplishments, succeeded in laying the foundation of an
enduring edifice: the organization of a group of young and eager
students who are devoted to a continuing joint study and investigation of psychoanalytical concepts in relation to their own
clinical experience. By placing it under the sponsorship of the
New York Psychoanalytic Institute, he made available facilities—
administrative aid, library, and experienced faculty—which would
not have been possible on an independent basis. He had nurtured
the early growth and development of this rebirth of traditional
approach and had watched over its ebullient growth to intellectual
maturity. Finally, in adapting the *modus operandi* of an over-
grown body in such fashion as to retain the advantage of a small
group, he had further extended its scope and usefulness. The later
reorganization of the group followed the ideas which Kris had
conceived before his death.

The presentations by the Arlow subgroup on ego regressions
in March and April, 1957, further validated the direction which
Kris had felt the activities of the group should take. Accordingly,
in May of 1957, at the final meeting of the year, specific recom-
mendations for further reorganization were discussed and subsequently presented for approval to the Educational Committee of
the Institute. A number of suggestions were considered in regard
to actions that the Study Group might undertake as a fitting tribute
to Ernst Kris. Among these was the designation of the reorganized
study group as the Ernst Kris Study Group.

In the reorganization the large group was divided into three
sections of approximately twenty participants each with Jacob A.
Arlow, Charles Brenner and Rudolph M. Loewenstein as the designated instructors or leaders. The previous membership had been

heterogeneous with respect to analytic experience, varying from fourth-year students to members of the Psychoanalytic Society of several years' standing. This feature was preserved in the otherwise arbitrary assignment of members to sections, since it was the consensus of the group that younger participants within each section should have the opportunity to benefit from the greater experience of older members. It seemed inappropriate to assign members of the faculty or senior members of the Society, who frequently sat in on the meetings, to a particular group. Instead, they were invited to attend and to participate in whichever activities of a section they might wish.

The purpose of the subdivision of the group was to facilitate discussion and to encourage participation by a greater number, but some meetings of the entire membership were envisioned for the purpose of hearing distinguished guests and receiving reports of its studies from each section. The reorganized study group was launched on September 26, 1957, in a particularly auspicious way by a combined meeting at which Miss Anna Freud discussed "Problems of Technique in Adult Analysis." During the academic year 1957-1958 the meetings of each individual section took on the quality of an analytic workshop in which there was continuing effort over several meetings to collect, collate, clarify, and even add to the available knowledge about a particular subject. At the first meeting of the sections in October 1957, Arlow's section chose for its topic "The Mechanism of Denial"; Brenner's section, "Factors Responsible for Success in Psychoanalytic Treatment"; and Loewenstein's section, "Indications for Psychoanalysis." In three additional meetings each section met individually to study its selected subject. Beginning in February 1958, there were combined meetings at which the sections reported their findings to the entire group.

The enthusiasm and devotion of the members of the study group to the intense and time-consuming studies resulted in unusually excellent reports and panel discussions at the combined meetings. The general interest aroused within the New York Psychoanalytic Society led its Program Committee to extend an invitation to the Kris Study Group to have one of its sections present a report of its year's study at the last meeting before the vacation period. On June 24, 1958, the Arlow Section gave a panel discussion on the results of its study of "The Mechanism of Denial." The invitation was again extended in 1959, and in subsequent years. A fourth section, under the leadership of David Beres, was added in 1961, and the study of each topic was extended over two years in order to allow time for more adequate development. A valuable feature of the earlier study group, the invitation of special guests from time to time, was reintroduced.

This brief history of the Ernst Kris Study Group demonstrates the gradual evolution of objectives, plans, and programs of the Group. Such flexibility is desirable if a group is to continue the process of adaptation to changing circumstances. Other groups, with similar objectives, will very likely have different situations, the requirements of which vary from those of the Kris Study Group. Nevertheless, some account of the present methodology of the Kris Study Group with respect to techniques and procedures may be useful to others who wish to form similar groups.

As is apparent from our experience, a well-led study group may grow to unwieldy proportions. The consequences, however, need not be disastrous. Subdivision of a large group into sections which may still meet conjointly on occasion has the advantage of enlisting greater individual participation and providing more informal discussion while maintaining a greater *esprit de corps*. The number of sections and leaders may be adjusted to the continuing growth of the organization. Membership of varied analytic experience came about spontaneously in our case and has worked well, but the size of a group and its make-up is often not a matter of choice. Reassignment of the sections to another leader each year has exposed the members to different personalities, different viewpoints and approaches to the common goal of collective study, At a later stage, after rotation of the sections among the instructors, a reshuffling of the membership of each section was tried. This change was thought to offer additional advantages, although it must be recognized that common interest and effort in a group fairly homogeneous as to ideals and standards may weld it into a well-integrated and efficiently functioning unit which should not be disturbed.

The indispensable role of a capable leader or leaders is self-evident, but a secretary is needed in addition. In the beginning of the study group one person was sufficient to confer with Kris on recommended reading and invitations to guests, and to send out notices for meetings. With the subdivision of the group into three sections, secretaries were found necessary for each section, and one of these[20] continued to serve that function for the group as a whole. When the activities of the Ernst Kris Study Group took on the nature of workshops, the secretary also served as a reporter after each meeting. However, the expansion of the activities of the Group soon made the manifold duties of the secretary too burdensome and additional help was required. The administrative staff of the Institute[21] had long ago assumed the task of mimeographing and mailing out notices of meetings, bibliographies, and clinical material, but other techniques had to be devised to distribute the work. These developed spontaneously from the suggestions of the group and were always undertaken on a voluntary basis. The meeting for the selection of the subjects to be studied and the planning of the year's program was shifted from the first meeting of the fall to the last meeting of the spring. This change gave more time to the leaders, secretaries, and other volunteers to compile a bibliography, review the literature, and find illustrative clinical material, so that the work of the group might start promptly each fall.

It has been our experience that careful reporting of each meeting is important, not only to preserve the content of the discussions but also as a stimulus to further thought prior to the next meeting. Without such a record, the subject may lie fallow until the next meeting, and discussion become repetitious. The reporting of a free discussion, however, is not an easy task. Even the few persons who have the required facility must often sacrifice their own participation for the task. Others find reporting extremely difficult, and this makes for considerable variation in quality. One section found it advantageous to record the entire discussion on tape and

---

[20] Dr. Bernard D. Fine has been the faithful and efficient secretary of the Group since its inception.

[21] Mr. Merrill H. Whitney, Executive Secretary of the New York Psychoanalytic Institute, and his staff have given invaluable assistance to the Group in handling the administrative details.

in the next year the other sections followed this example. Though a verbatim transcription of the recording is undesirably long and loses continuity, a detailed summary may be easily prepared from the tape. A different volunteer undertook this task after each meeting, thereby spreading the work load. It was found that those who undertook this chore were amply rewarded and became enthusiastic participants at the next meeting. The work which they carried out as a responsibility to the entire group resulted in an increased cathexis with respect to the subject matter, leading to additional contributions of their own.

The summaries of each session are also of invaluable aid in the preparation of the final reports on each subject which are presented to the entire Kris Study Group. These reports are the responsibility of a committee of four to six active participants who also constitute the panel to whom questions are directed during the combined meetings. They hold separate meetings with the leader to select, clarify, and organize the most significant contributions. Often this task has been so stimulating that it required several two-hour sessions and became a valuable extension of the study group. One section committee chose to have a single individual, with the assistance of a colleague, prepare a systematic resume of the deliberations of the section. It was felt that this procedure would facilitate the integration of the material and give unity to the report. It was always true, however, that spheres of special interest emerged among the committee members, and these often formed the basis for the assignment of parts of the report to separate persons, a plan followed by other sections. Prior to a combined meeting, the report from the section committee is circulated to the entire membership. With such preparation, discussion can begin immediately after an introduction by the chairman or after only brief statements of their points of view by members of the panel.

That the ego ideals of members of a group are significantly influenced by contact with a brilliant and stimulating teacher is neither a new discovery nor unique to psychoanalysis. The Ernst Kris Study Group demonstrates, however, the means by which the inspiration of such a man continues to be utilized in an organized fashion for the advancement of study and training. Helene Deutsch (1940) says: "One thing remained, however, which gave to the Vienna group up to its final days a wholly personal stamp: tradition. This tradition continued to be preserved for several years —perhaps the pleasantest and most serene ones—through the personal contact with Freud in those monthly meetings in which Freud communicated to the small select group his new ideas or amplified and corrected his older ones." She adds, "History repeats itself." The Ernst Kris Study Group continues the intellectually rewarding tradition of its earlier psychoanalytic predecessors.

BIBLIOGRAPHY

Bornstein, B. (1959), personal communication.
Brill, A. A. (1938), Introduction. In: *The Basic Writings of Sigmund Freud*. New York: Modern Library.
Buxbaum, E. (1951), Freud's Dream Interpretation in the Light of His Letters to Fliess. *Bull. Menninger Clin.*, 15:197-212.
Deutsch, H. (1940), Freud and His Pupils: A Footnote to the History of the Psychoanalytic Movement. *Psychoanal. Quart.*, 9:184-194.
Federn, E. (1960), personal communication.
Freud, S. (1887-1902), *The Origins of Psychoanalysis. Letters to Wilhelm Fliess, Drafts and Notes, 1887-1902*. London: Imago, 1954.
―――― (1914), The History of the Psychoanalytic Movement. *Standard Edition*, 14:3-66. London: Hogarth Press, 1957.
―――― (1921), Group Psychology and the Analysis of the Ego. *Standard Edition*, 18:69-143. London: Hogarth Press, 1955.
Hartmann, H. (1959), personal communication.
Hendrick, I. (1961), *The Birth of an Institute*. Freeport, Maine: Bond Wheelwright.
Jacobson, E. (1959), personal communication.
Jones, E. (1955), *The Life and Work of Sigmund Freud*, 2. New York: Basic Books.
Karpe, R. (1960), personal communication.
Kris, M. (1959), personal communication.
Lewin, B. D. (1959), personal communication.
―――― and Ross, H. (1960), *Psychoanalytic Education in the United States*. New York: Norton.
New York Psychoanalytic Institute (1953). Minutes of the Curriculum Committee.
―――― (1953-1954), *Catalogue of the New York Psychoanalytic Institute*.
Nunberg, H. and Federn, E. (1962), *The Minutes of the Vienna Psychoanalytic Society*, 1. New York: International Universities Press.
Oberndorf, C. P. (1927), History of the Psychoanalytic Movement in America. *Psychoanal. Rev.*, 14:3.
―――― (1953), *A History of Psychoanalysis in America*. New York: Grune & Stratton.
Spiegel, L. A. (1963), personal communication.

Beating Fantasies

EDWARD D. JOSEPH, M.D., *Reporter*

Participants: Herbert Aldendorff, M.D.—Leon L. Altman, M.D.—
Jacob A. Arlow, M.D.—Stuart Asch, M.D.—Ted E. Becker, M.D.—
Charles Brenner, M.D.—Bernard Brodsky, M.D.—Kenneth T. Calder,
M.D.—John Donadeo, M.D.—Ellis Feer, M.D.—Bernard D. Fine, M.D.
—Jules Glenn, M.D.—Merl Jackel, M.D.—Edward D. Joseph, M.D.
—Arnold Kallen, M.D.—William P. Kapuler, M.D.—Louis Kaywin,
M.D.—Edward Kloth, M.D.—Ernst Kris, M.D.—Mathew Levine, M.D.
—Leo S. Loomie, Jr., M.D.—Betty Magruder, M.D.—Ernest Marcus,
M.D.—John B. McDevitt, M.D.— Burness E. Moore, M.D.—Werner
Nathan, M.D.—William G. Niederland, M.D.—Eugene Nininger, M.D.
—Joshua M. Perman, M.D.—Arnold Z. Pfeffer, M.D.—Samuel Ritvo,
M.D.—David L. Rubinfine, M.D.—Oscar Sachs, M.D.—Jay Schorr,
M.D.—Irwin Solomon, M.D.—Rebecca G. Solomon, M.D.—Jacob E.
Stump, M.D.—Herbert F. Waldhorn, M.D.—Philip Weissman, M.D.
—George H. Wiedeman, M.D.

THE SUBJECT OF BEATING fantasies was considered by the Kris
Study Group in two sessions, a month apart. The first meeting was
preceded by the presentation of case material gathered by a small
panel of the Group, meeting under the leadership of Dr. Charles
Brenner. The purpose of the panel, in meeting in advance, had
been to pave the way so that the time and attention of the entire

Group would not be taken up by presentation of clinical material; but rather that the Group could proceed to further considerations on the basis of known clinical data.

The members of the panel introduced their contribution with the statement: "The subject of beating fantasies is a subtopic under the heading of sadomasochism on the one hand, and under the heading of fantasies in mental life on the other, in particular the influence of childhood masturbatory fantasies on later psychic development, both normal and neurotic." They brought the following illustrative case material, drawn from their practices, to the Study Group for discussion.

Case 1

With this patient, a man of thirty-six, the fantasy of being beaten occurred for the first time one and a half years after he entered analysis. One day, while walking on the street, he saw a mother spank her disobedient child on the buttocks. While witnessing the scene he not only *fantasied,* but also *wished* to be spanked in a similar way by this woman. In talking about this event he recalled the occasional spanking he received from his mother when he disobeyed her. Further association brought to mind the time when he grew too big for his mother to administer corporal punishment, and she would call upon the boarder in their home, a big policeman (the oedipal father), to punish him. One time, when he was especially naughty toward his mother, this man gave him a thrashing on the buttocks. Even though he knew that his mother could call upon Pepe, the boarder, to punish him, he would provoke her, usually by hitting her in the abdomen. When it was suggested that his provocation of his mother was motivated by an unconscious wish to be beaten by Pepe, the patient was at first somewhat amazed, yet credulous. This interpretation opened the way toward the exploration of his latent homosexual problem. The patient, whose father was a weak man, would have liked him to be strong and forceful like Pepe.

This patient indulged in a sadistic perversion which consisted in sex play involving a couple, usually husband and wife. The husband would sit on the floor in the corner of the room while the patient would whip the man's wife, not hard enough to inflict injury, but just enough to make her cry out in pain. In the back of the patient's mind was always the question, why did the husband let him get away with it. The patient also visited prostitutes who would allow him to administer token thrashings. This enabled him to function as a potent male in the sexual act.

The analysis was not completed. However, on the basis of the material obtained, a plausible hypothesis is that the beating the patient administered to the woman was a means of calling down upon himself the real beating which he unconsciously desired from the father. The woman would cry out for his father (the boarder) to come and beat him. In one sense the perversion may have been an acting out of the means of obtaining this wish. The sadism here appeared to be only a means to a masochistic end. As far as his beating fantasy was concerned, the patient's conscious wish was to be beaten by the woman. In actuality, in the perversion, the opposite occurred: he beat the woman. As Freud pointed out, in the conscious fantasy of the male, the unconscious wish has to be denied by changing the sex of the one who administers the beating. In this case, it seems the perversion served as a means of carrying out the unconscious wish to be beaten.

Undoubtedly both fantasy and perversion in this case are highly overdetermined, but in terms of the patient's negative oedipal wishes, this case followed closely the lines laid down by Freud (1919) in his paper, "A Child Is Being Beaten."

The question might be raised as to the reason for request for the beating. The term "request" is used advisedly, because the "request" may not be synonymous with the "wish." In other words, the beating may not be desired in and for itself, but rather in lieu of a greater danger, i.e., castration. Furthermore, if the beating wish involves baring the buttocks, might this not be the sacrifice of the buttocks for the penis? In the case of this patient, a confession would occur from time to time. (Incidentally, this patient was an imposter, and therefore always had much to confess at his disposal.) He would feel better after confession, i.e., there was a lessening of his anxiety. It seemed as if he gained immunity, as it were, after the confession. What proved to be the case was that by confessing he was submitting himself to the analyst for a reprimand in lieu of a much greater punishment, viz., being exposed as a castrated person, or being exposed to castration (revealed as "insane" or exposed as a charlatan). The confession was a saving distraction. By confessing in the analysis, he banked upon his contrition, thus appealing to the analyst's loving kindness and forgivingness, and placing him in the role of a powerful father. The speculation, then, is that the confession and the request for a beating may both be traced back to a belief that these are means of obtaining immunity from castration.

Case 2

The patient is a tall, gaunt, twenty-eight-year-old man with a tortured and woebegone expression. He is stoop-shouldered and speaks in a grave voice never varying in expression or intonation. There is frequent twitching of head, arms, and trunk. He came for treatment because of an inability to study or to complete the examinations necessary to his profession. There are "blocked-up" sensations in his head, complaints of impotence, premature ejaculations, and depression.

His father is perfectionistic, capable, popular, and a highly regarded professional. He is worrisome and became distraught at the patient's older sister's childhood temper tantrums and behavior disorders. At those times he threatened and attempted without success to beat her in order to make her behave. The patient sympathized with the parents against his sister's behavior and wanted father to punish her by beating. In later years the sister married after a successful analysis. The patient is unmarried and was encouraged to enter analysis by his sister. The mother favored him over his sister but decried the tendency of both to go their own way.

As a child, the patient was always dour. This was noticed by the family and others. He had only male companions in adolescence, and suffered from an inability to have girl friends. He was distant, aloof, and brooding at home and with his family or their friends. Later, he selected girls for dates only under an inner compulsion to "have sex," but without affect. He recreated the sisterly relation with them and treated them as he had treated his sister. The first outright difficulty was in college, where he could not continue his studies. He became depressed and had father come to take him away for therapy.

Beating Fantasies and Practices

(a) "I am tied up while a woman dances naked in front of me; I can't screw her. I am released and proceed to screw her while she beats me. Water is put on to make it hurt more and be more exciting." (b) "I beat myself on the buttocks with paddles to give myself an erection before masturbating." (c) "I beat a woman on the behind and she slaps me or I slap myself." (d) "I go to the movies to see women being beaten, also men being beaten."

Course of Analysis

After considering, but eliminating, the possibility of psychosis, the diagnosis was severe obsessive-compulsive character disorder with depression. The manifestations were marked ambivalence, ruminating doubts, indecisiveness, "yes-and-no" debates with himself over everything, inability to make up his mind, and miserliness. There were bizarre somatic and hypochondriacal symptoms—"get tight all over, tightening in head, just tighten up." Besides the beating fantasies, he had obsessive ideas of "eating shit" or "spitting in your face." Transference reactions were marked by a profound ambivalence alternating from servile deference to withering contempt. He showed a defensive shyness with timidity, withdrawal, and inability to do anything, accompanied by, or shifting to, megalomanic, narcissistic fantasies of magical omnipotence and superiority. He had a ritual compulsion to touch or "sip water," "or else something bad will happen." Homosexual dreams were numerous with special emphasis on transference manifestations.

The genetic development of his beating fantasies came from the relation to sister and father—replacing sister-mother and assuming a passive-feminine role with father (father beats him as he would sister). The beating fantasies also represent homosexual wishes in relation to other men and serve as a defense against oedipal wishes. Multiple anal derivatives were displayed in his character structure, fantasies, and masturbatory activities. Libidinization of the superego and masochistic ego defenses were a prominent feature.

Illustrative Verbatim Material

"In masturbating, I groan and moan, hold it in and back until it hurts; it feels good that way. I feel I should make myself depressed, tighten up, make myself upset. Taking a shit, I feel I have to look at it, my head tightens up then, and I must tense up."

"I keep my hands at my side here because I might want to touch my penis. I'm afraid you will touch it or attack me. I want a girl to touch my penis and jerk me off. I writhe around when masturbating to get the feeling of agony and suffering with an erection. Whenever I'm feeling good, I have to stop and think and tighten up with the thought of having to suffer about something."

"Frequently have a fantasy of shitting in my pants in public or snorting, grimacing and twitching." The latter is an actual daily occurrence in analytic sessions.

"I can make my head feel 'lumpy.' I go to the bathroom to be alone, and get the tensed-up, heavy, tight feeling."

"When I think of beating myself or the girl slapping me, I groan and call her name but want it to go on. Groaning and moaning is part of the pleasure of the pain."

Case 3

The patient is a thirty-one-year-old, single man. He had had six months of psychotherapy and stated that his reason for coming was that he had a "fetish." The fetish originally involved blue denim overalls, but in recent years he has also found dungarees exciting. He would seek every opportunity of seeing young men in dungarees. The excitement would be heightened if the patient himself were in dungarees. He would then stand near the other man and hope that the man would notice that the patient had dungarees on. Occasionally he would put on dungarees and a work shirt and look at himself in the mirror, concentrating on the buttocks and profile. Frequently this led to masturbation or was accompanied by it. However, in the patient's most frequent masturbatory fantasy, he thinks of a stern father figure, usually a farmer, and therefore wearing overalls. This man is beating or spanking his son, who is also in overalls, on the covered buttocks. He likes to make the son as old as seems reasonable—twelve or fifteen years of age. Sometimes, in the fantasy, the patient takes the father's role, sometimes the son's. In other masturbatory fantasies he is telling people about this hypothetical stern father, how he made the patient go to work at an early age, and mistreated and beat him.

At times the patient responds to newspaper advertisements for stockboy in a grocery store. He is stimulated by talking to the prospective employer about working long hours, doing hard work for little pay. While talking to him on the telephone, he is sexually excited and frequently masturbates. As soon as he ejaculates, he is repelled by what he is doing and hangs up. He has, on two or three occasions, acted out the fantasy by taking menial jobs as a dishwasher or in a fruit and vegetable market. However, he does not stay more than one hour or so before he loses interest and quits. He has also acted out his beating fantasy on himself. Standing in front of the mirror in his dungarees and work shirt, he hits himself lightly on the buttocks with a strap. He has an almost delusional fear that the neighbors will hear him do it, and always turns the television set on loudly at such times. If he "inadvertently" hits hard enough to hurt himself, he thinks, "What the hell am I doing to myself?" and immediately stops.

The patient is an only child of Jewish parents. His father is a tailor, a fact which the patient's mother instructed him not to mention.

Although of very superior intelligence, the patient did only average work at school but did manage to obtain a Master's degree in vocational guidance. He has an undemanding civil service job in that field. In childhood, he was a severe stutterer and still, at times, shows hesitation in speech.

The patient rarely free-associates and acknowledges that he is consciously withholding. About a year after the analysis started, he said that he still slept in his parents' bedroom. Only a few months ago, he stated that it is not rare for his mother to come into the bathroom to urinate while he is taking a bath. "I did not want to tell you because you would make something of it," the patient said. His attitudes are further exemplified by the following: Some years ago, the patient was panicked when he noticed a lesion on his penis. He thought it might be cancer. For months he refrained from looking at his penis again. When, at last, he could no longer tolerate the anxiety and went to a doctor, there was nothing there.

On the job, the patient pretends to be a man about town who takes out the most glamorous girls only. In fact, he has had no overt sexual experiences with either sex. He has great difficulty describing his masturbatory activity. It seems certain that he does not touch the bare penis. He puts his hand alongside the penis, touching the groin through his shorts. He finds it even more difficult to talk about his attitudes to bowel movements and feces than to talk about masturbation. Coprophilic impulses and defenses against them are hinted at.

The patient's earliest memory dates back to about age five, when a little boy was coming to play with him. Either the boy had overalls on or the patient did, and the patient changed to match the other boy. He remembers, at eleven, playing father and son with another boy and that, in pretending to spank the other boy, he became sexually aroused. He also remembers hitting himself with a brush. At first these were separated from masturbation, which the patient did *not* regard as "sexual." The patient has occasionally had transvestite fantasies and has put on lipstick and make-up and looked at himself in the mirror.

So far the understanding of this case is limited. The dungarees clearly represent masculinity and, at one level, the penis. When standing next to a man in dungarees, the patient thinks, "Look at me. I am a man like you," or, "I am like you," or, "Look at me. I work. I am a man." It would seem then that the patient is seeking to deny his feminine identification by identifying himself with a masculine figure.

The beating is not something to be taken seriously, but is a kind of token beating, actually representing a form of love. Dreams and associations have expressed the idea that a good father punishes his son. At other times there have been hints that the beatings also represent punishment for defiant attitudes to the father. In the transference, the patient shows a pseudo nonchalant attitude which covers great fear of the analyst who is pictured as strict, punitive, and cold.

The beating fantasies have undergone two significant changes: 1. On rare occasions, the patient fantasies being beaten on the bare buttocks. 2. He is occasionally stimulated by the story of a woman beating her child, either boy or girl, and masturbates while thinking of this event.

Case 4

The patient is a twenty-six-year-old biochemist who has been in analysis for approximately three years. He complained of feelings of depression, lack of satisfaction with what he was doing, and inability to work. In the course of the analysis, he has succeeded in obtaining his doctorate and doing what seems to be original work in his field.

Early in his analysis it became evident that his whole life and his relations with people were governed by his creating situations, with both men and women, in which he or someone close to him was being beaten. Characteristic of this were frequent incidents in his work in which he broke laboratory apparatus or spoiled an experiment, bringing down the wrath of his supervisor upon himself or his co-worker. The most flagrant example which unfolded over a period of months was a situation in which he first introduced his girl friend to a younger brother. He then encouraged the girl to respond to the younger brother's advances. He made it possible for them to be together on many occasions, absenting himself with rationalized excuses, thus creating a favorable situation for the brother and the girl friend to have an affair. He isolated and denied his knowledge that this was going on, and managed to surprise them both in his apartment, seemingly without any warning or advance knowledge that there was anything occurring. His reaction to this sudden revelation was to beat up his brother and the girl. He could be restrained only by their combined efforts. Less flagrant examples of this had occurred in previous relationships with women in which he would be very insulting, arrogant, and sadistic in his behavior until they were sufficiently angered to tell him off. These situations with girls always occurred in relationship to other boy friends.

A similar relationship existed between him and his parents, particularly the father. Frequently, through a "mishap" on the patient's part, he brought the father's wrath upon himself. Equally, in the transference, he has often tried to provoke the analyst. On occasion, he has exclaimed that he doesn't understand how the analyst can stand his behavior and thoughts, or why and how it is that the analyst doesn't get angry at him. There have been fantasies that this occurred.

Early in the analysis, one of his many recurrent memories emerged. This was of his standing on the stairs and watching his father, usually a meek, mild man, viciously beating the dog, generally for soiling the rug, and enjoying the punishment being meted out. Some time later, associations came out of how he, the patient, would get his younger brother into trouble with the family so that the younger brother would be punished, usually by a spanking.

His earliest memory, which he dated back to the age of eighteen months, was of being held up to a large window to see his mother and father coming down the road during a thunderstorm, and of his being intensely afraid that they would be struck by lightning. His association to this memory invariably involves the frequent enemas which he was given by a nurse at that early age, and later, through childhood, by his mother. Apparently, he slept in the parents' bedroom until the age of four or five, although there is no memory of this other than his having been told it. He does know, however, that he was a breath-holder until that age, a habit which wreaked havoc with the household until it was suddenly terminated by the parents plunging him, during one of these episodes, into a bath of cold water.

Subsequently, in relation to both the dog and the brother, it became clear that he actually had gotten them both into the situations in which they would be punished, the dog by the severe beatings, the brother by lesser punishments, while he himself would look on with feelings of intense pleasure, excitement, and guilt.

Conscious masturbation has been denied consistently. He has recalled many a time lying in bed, holding his whole body tense, guarding against any sort of erotic fantasy. However, this often did not quite succeed, for it has come out that, in spite of this intense bodily rigidity and extreme control, he would begin to get an erection. Then, his final attempt at control would be a fantasy in which his penis would be rolling along a conveyor belt, going through a rolling mill press, and then dropping into a boiling cauldron of molten metal at the end of the conveyor belt. This fantasy invariably terminated whatever degree of erection he had. Parenthetically, his father was the supervisor of a rolling mill.

He has always conceived of intercourse as a man attacking a woman.

While there is doubt in his mind that he witnessed the primal scene, he knows that during those times when he would lie in bed, rigidly, attempting to control himself, he could overhear sounds from his parents' bedroom, sounds which to him were of intercourse, that is, of a vicious attack in which father was beating mother verbally or physically.

The borderline between this patient's living out a beating fantasy in relation to himself, his brother, and their various substitutes, and a masochistic attitude and relationship with people is a very thin one. There is no doubt of the extreme pleasure and gratification that he feels in situations in which he or a close male is at the receiving end of some form of beating. The actual content of the beating fantasy that was so rigidly repressed and controlled, even to the extent of the extreme castration fantasy, has not yet unfolded.

It should be added that another of the patient's symptoms is rigid and tense body musculature, resembling Parkinson's disease. This is a defense against intense aggressive drives and resembles as well the body tenseness used to control masturbatory fantasies. A body-phallus equation seems involved also, so that the beatings are a source of libidinal gratification.

Case 5

The patient is a thirty-nine-year-old unmarried woman scientist who came to analysis because of feelings of depression and a general sense of dissatisfaction with her life. The decision to seek analysis followed the breaking off of a three-year relationship with a married man who had regularly promised to divorce his wife and marry the patient, but was unable to carry through this plan.

The first of two children, the patient came from a middle European family. Father was a small businessman who earned a moderately good living. He was a very gentle, passive man who doted on the patient. The mother was also a very kindly, gentle, but rather timid person. Neither parent was able to control or discipline the patient who was a stubborn, headstrong, extremely aggressive child. When there was any conflict, the parents simply gave in, unable to cope with her screaming temper tantrums. One of the patient's earliest memories has to do with the intensity with which she insisted on doing things for and by herself. Her earliest recollection of speech involved a repetition of the words, "I, my self."

On rare occasions, mother would threaten punishment by brandishing a belt. This produced such panic in the patient that she screamed uncontrollably and mother would be rendered helpless. She wondered why she was so panic-stricken, since she was never punished or beaten. The patient also recalled that until the age of four she was allowed to crawl into bed with her mother after father left for work. There she would play with mother's breasts. At the age of four, mother put a sudden stop to this. She reacted very violently and remembered dreaming that mother was dead but her breasts were hanging on a hook in the patient's room.

Around this same time, she suffered from nightmares in which she was chased by witches. Also, on falling asleep, she would have an image of a woman rolling a huge, empty barrel that produced a thundering noise. (This later proved to be a condensation product deriving from later experiences having to do with mother's pregnancy plus an association of flatus and primal scene noises.) This was accompanied by sensations of thickness, stiffness and increase in size of the hands, tongue, and mouth. (This had a phallic meaning as well as representing an identification with her nursing brother.)

Father played a guitar and, from the age of six, the patient remembered him playing for mother. Once, following such a serenade, she jumped on and smashed the guitar. Father reacted with hurt and puzzlement and never played again. There was also a memory of wanting father to burn a hole in the rear end of a doll with his cigarette.

There were many memories of struggles with a governess over whether the patient should urinate prior to their daily walks. The patient would invariably win such contests and refuse to urinate. Also, invariably, when they were outdoors, she insisted she had to urinate and a frantic search would ensue for a public washroom. Once, when the governess finally refused to look for a washroom, the patient had the humiliating experience of wetting her pants in a shop. Another pertinent memory from this period had to do with a sexual overture from a female schoolmate in the school washroom. There was mutual touching of buttocks. Subsequently this girl visited the patient in her home and there is a vivid recollection of waiting in horrified excitement for this friend to tell the patient's parents about the sexual play. Of course, this did not occur.

Childhood masturbation was screened by a memory cathected with intense shame of picking mucus from her nose while in bed and rubbing it on the wall. There were also many fantasies and dreams of presenting an adult man (father) with her buttocks and having a huge bowel movement. Her school adjustment during this time (she attended a Catholic school) was characterized by excellent work, rebellion against restriction (she was a leader of rebellion) and by intense tomboy activities in competition with boys.

When she was ten years old, a brother was born. While mother was at the hospital, the patient contracted scarlet fever and had to be kept in isolation with a nurse. Thus when mother and infant came home, the mother could not attend the patient and could only see her from a distance. The patient recalled how, on one occasion, she insisted hysterically on handling a gift brought by friends for the baby, although she realized that she was contaminating the object so that the baby could not have it.

On her recovery, she remembered feelings of possessiveness toward and fondness for the brother. There was, at this time, a character change in her with the development of strong reaction formations. She became more sedate and extremely studious. She developed intellectual and moral preoccupations concerning good and evil and constructed ethical systems. She became "father's girl," delighting him with her intellectual interests which he encouraged. Occasionally, there was a return of the repressed in sadistic behavior toward her brother while ostensibly teaching him. She would make him sit immobile and repeat things till he wept. Or she would suddenly decide to stop giving a local beggar alms because she was deriving too great a sense of pride and self-satisfaction from it. She decided to study law.

In adolescence, she developed several very intense attachments to girl friends whom she considered prettier and more attractive to boys than she. While these girls were dating, she studied harder. She did have a fantasy crush on a boy who never knew of it, and felt that her love life was over when he migrated with his family to another country. Starting in adolescence and continuing to the time of her analysis, she masturbated (either with thigh pressure or rubbing against the bed) with a fantasy that she was *observing* a woman, trussed, bound and face down, buttocks exposed, being beaten and/or raped by an unidentified man. Frequently this man would invite a younger man to view or participate. Pain played *no* part in the fantasy. The patient was always an onlooker.

It became clear in the analysis, from transference material, that at age seven, following an emergency appendectomy in which she was frightened by the rough surgeon, the outlines of the subsequent fantasy were formed with herself as the victim. It is significant that, following the operation, the patient developed a transient dog phobia (fear of dogs biting her), which vanished after a dream in which she mastered a dangerous black dog who became submissive to her.

She also fantasied wandering around the world alone and friendless, with no money and in rags, but triumphant and vibrantly alive. She practiced law briefly after receiving her degree, but began to feel she had to get away from home or be strangled. She found her own apartment, but then suddenly decided to migrate to the United States at the age of twenty-one. Just prior to leaving, she had a "horrible" dream in which her mother forced her to submit to intercourse with her father. Once here, she survived by working at a series of factory jobs. Despite her fears, she forced herself in a counterphobic manner to have intercourse with several men in succession, all of them of the weak, passive variety. She found she could enjoy intercourse in the superior position, but did not experience orgasm.

The patient was married briefly to a weak, ineffectual man who was unable to find work and lived on her earnings. After several years of "anesthesia and then growing desperation," she decided she wanted to return to school. Characteristically, she literally sloughed off her old life, including her husband, aggressively arranged a scholarship (through the generosity of a wealthy woman) and began to study. Very quickly, she was recognized as an unusually gifted and creative person by her teachers.

During this time the Nazis came to power and she learned that her family had been destroyed, probably in the gas chambers. She was not noticeably depressed but fantasied murdering and destroying Nazi stormtroopers. There was some guilt because she had, for several years previously, been haunted by the fear that her parents and brother would come here and she would have to give up her studies to take care of them.

After the war, she was granted a fellowship to study in Israel and lived there for a year, going through many harrowing and dangerous experiences occasioned by the Arab wars, again bolstered by counterphobic defenses. While in Israel, she attempted to locate her brother, on the small chance that he was among the children who had been rescued.

It was on her return that she met and began a three-year relationship with a married man with two children. This man had been a political prisoner of the Nazis and had narrowly escaped the gas chamber. However, his first wife had been executed after being overcome with masochistic paralysis of will when she had the opportunity to escape. The man had remarried. The patient became fascinated by the story of the first wife and actually corresponded with European friends in an effort to learn more details of her character and concentration camp experience. She mourned this woman with all the intensity she had not been able to experience over her parents' death. The lover kept promising to divorce his wife and marry the patient, but was unable to go through with this. There were frequent, violent quarrels and ecstatic reconciliations. The sexual adjustment was as previously described, with the addition of especially warm feelings for her partner's penis which she fondled and personified.

She had transient depressions during the three-year period which she did not recognize as such, and there were occasional obsessive thoughts of piercing her eye with rusty nails. In 1953, she began to steal small, inconsequential items from department stores, experiencing a great sense of exhilaration. In 1954, she was apprehended by a store detective and brought to the company offices where she was warned and released. She was panic-stricken by this "narrow escape" and never stole again. She became depressed, realized at this point the emptiness of her relationship with her lover, and also began to feel she had not progressed in her work because of difficulty in writing and publishing papers. Through the influence of and financial aid from an older female colleague, she sought analysis.

Course of Analysis

It was typical of this patient in the opening phase of the analysis that, on her first telephone contact with the analyst, she exuberantly said, "I am so glad we are having an analysis together." Almost immediately she took the reins and galloped off, dreaming profusely, analyzing her dreams, and producing childhood memories. There was rarely even a momentary pause, and she came prepared for every hour. She would pay her fee before the analyst could present her with statements; this was accompanied by vivid anal dreams. It is accurate to say that her treatment proved to be an analysis of her beating fantasies in all their overdetermined ramifications.

The analyst began gradually to interpret her defense of taking over the analysis, preparing in advance for each hour, and attempting to anticipate any interpretation from him, and made her aware that she must be afraid of what might happen otherwise. Also, her need to observe him carefully—how he said things, what he seemed to find important—was seen first as a wish to emulate and be like him and then as a wish to steal something from him. At this time the story of her stealing emerged. She became depressed and tearful, and developed somatic symptoms. She complained that the analyst did not like her. She developed urinary urgency and had to interrupt her hours to go to the washroom.

With irresistible force, she experienced for the first time the full force of her grief, guilt, and horror over the loss of her parents and brother. When this storm had waned, she dreamed violent dreams of seducing, castrating, and driving men to suicide. Alternately, she dreamed of sitting at an open window, bathed in the setting sun, with her wrists gashed and her blood ebbing away. For the first time in her life, she became overtly depressed and sick prior to and during her menstrual periods, and dreamed of forcing men to see her ugliness and messiness. These dreams accompanied her first sexual feelings in the transference.

The first change in her beating fantasies now occurred: she found herself identified with the second man. This was also punctuated by profuse primal scene material in dreams, and by voyeuristic fantasies of seeing me in the washroom urinating or masturbating. She began to understand how the frustration of her initial attempt to identify herself with the analyst (and, at a deeper level, to rob him of his penis) had mobilized severe anxiety. As a result of the frustration, the underlying penis envy, rage, and castrative impulses then emerged, and when this had been worked through in the transference and in her oedipal conflicts, she began to express her desire for a child from the analyst.

The screen memory of her mother's breasts shed its regressive form and reemerged genitally as rage with father for giving mother the baby she wanted, as well as her own phallic wish to replace her father. The memory of smashing his guitar emerged here. She acted out her wish to become pregnant in a transient affair and managed to suppress her menses for several weeks, giving herself a good scare.

She began to write papers which were received enthusiastically in her field and wrote a long-deferred book on her studies in Israel. At this time, she masturbated with the fantasy that she was walking with the analyst in an idyllic, romantic setting, longing to submit sexually, when suddenly a threatening, dangerous man appeared. She kicked him in the groin. The analyst was repelled and lost interest in her. Her deep masochistic fantasies with all the accompanying vivid castration anxiety emerged in connection with her feminine positive oedipal wishes. Mother emerged as warm, loving, and understanding, rather than as stupid, dull, and insensitive. As a last resort, she turned desperately to her female friends, getting involved in their problems, and demanding that the analyst see them in consultation.

She dreamed at this point that she was being pursued through a forest by a man with a club. She came to a stream whereupon, removing some structure from her mouth, she could float across the stream to safety. There, in a house, she wrote books. Here, in describing the dream, she wanted to say she achieved "meteoric fame" but could not think of the word, so she substituted "astronomic"—however, she made a slip and said instead "gastronomic" fame. The interpretation of this dream brought out the regressive, oral, homosexual wishes which defended her against her penis envy and masochistic genital fantasies, as well as the envy of her nursing brother to which she had reacted in her febrile state (scarlet fever) with Isakower experiences.

She became more feminine and softer in appearance, manner, and dress. Men in her department began to notice and compliment her. Her fantasies, for the first time, were of having intercourse with a man, and she found the idea of being underneath exciting. A termination date was set with a flare-up of rage, penis envy, and obsessive thoughts of piercing her eyes with sharp instruments, and then depression. These things were worked through in terms of termination, uneventfully.

Summary of Latent Content of Beating Fantasy

(1) The patient is watching mother and father have intercourse. (2) She is the second man invited to participate with father in sexual assault on mother. (3) As a man she has the desired penis. (4) She is the child invited to participate with the parents in their sexual activity. (5) She is the victim (mother) having intercourse with father. (6) Bound and helpless, she is not accountable to her superego for her oedipal wishes. (7) The anal regression protects her against castration anxiety.

Case 6

This case is that of a highly masochistic twenty-six-year-old girl who has been acting out ideas of punishment and humiliation during her analysis by coming very late and provoking the analyst in many ways. The entire analysis has been treated as a humiliating experience. Confession of her failures has formed a large part of the associations. Her relationship to her mother (and the major part of the transference) was always centered about who was making whom suffer, worry, wait, do for. There were conscious memories of the transformation of these ideas of suffering into a positive attribute. Father would lay down the law and when she was very little would spank her on the buttocks—but even a gesture was enough. With mother, however, it was different; she could spank her and spank her but she would come back for more.

In the analysis, after it was pointed out to her that she was deriving certain satisfactions from her "suffering," and that it fitted in with her "strength through adversity" ideas, she told of her masturbation fantasies. The fantasies were repeated ones of being beaten and tortured. In what appears to be their order of evolution they are: (a) ideas of being beaten (spanked). (b) "Hanging by my thumbs stretched from head to toe, beaten but never killed ... to the point of unbearable pain ... but not enough to kill. ..." On questioning, it appeared that this fantasy had to do with one man. (c) "Concentration camp fantasies. ... A man or a few men with sadistic eyes strap me down to a table with the ideas of beating and torture ... there was a lot of sexual stuff too but kind of mixed up." In preparation, sometimes a machine or a hand would be used (to masturbate her) and she would become so aroused she would be "dying from it." A variation of this fantasy was of her being tied to a stake and many men "using" her. (d) The later fantasy was a rescue fantasy which, from later material, was related to her hearing of an actual similar event when she was about six years old. "Knocked down by a car . . . a man comes and takes me to the hospital, visits me often and falls in love with me" ... but she looks so beaten up in the mornings.

These fantasies show the progress of her displacement from the original object (mother) to the father (one man) who is then concealed by ideas of many men. The sexual ideas are also on the anal-sadistic level. Her identification with the man and her intense aggression toward him (of which there is much other evidence) are also shown in the projection that they are stimulating her but "leaving her hanging"—an expression which she frequently uses and which has both an oral and a genital meaning.

The final fantasy, which emerged months later, related to a story about her cousin, which she heard when she was about six years old. She remembers admiring him greatly. The woman he married after "rescuing" her could not have any children, and so two were adopted. The patient believes that the sterility was caused by an injury. During the analysis, she had a great desire to become pregnant which was related also to a fear of being sterile. The idea of the hospital also was related to the wish for a baby, after "injury."

Case 7

The patient is a young man of twenty-nine who came to analysis because of his social anxieties (he was a teacher) and his inability to complete his doctoral thesis. He had the idea that he would be forced to do the necessary work. Essentially, he was passive and had strong latent homosexual conflicts. These had been worked through to some extent when the fantasy in question was related in analysis.

The hour began with his saying that he had not wanted to come. After some time, he mentioned masturbating the night before but gave no details, thus making the analyst ask him to tell more about it. The fantasy was based on an article the patient had been reading about spanking and the existence of clubs in which this perversion is practiced.

He goes or is taken to the club as a visitor, where he meets a number of women who seem to be quite eager for him to spank them. This would then be followed by intercourse, a tergo.

He ignores these women however and approaches a girl who is hiding in the background, who protests in some way (saying she is also a visitor?). He realizes that this is a pretense and insists upon spanking her on the bare buttocks.

He mentioned the magazine article, and also some other stories he had heard about. This led to memories of his being jealous of his older brother when mother had beaten him across the legs with a rod.

From this fantasy, the transference elements and his own identification with the woman were shown to him. It also became possible to reexamine the exhibitionistic and voyeuristic elements. Further primal scene material was also obtained.

Case 8

This fragment of a case history is presented essentially to recount the recovery of an early beating fantasy which was acted out in play in childhood, but which seems to have left little in the way of permanent neurotic results. The patient, who has been in analysis for three months, is a twenty-six-year-old businessman, intensely ambitious and hard-working, who came to analysis on the insistence of his parents. This followed the successful therapy of his older sister.

The sibling rivalry with sister (six years older) has always been intense, but tempered with a great deal of love and devotion. His main symptoms are in the field of sexuality. He had only had intercourse three times prior to analysis, each time with a different woman. Frequent opportunities were denied, and he would just avoid seeing girl friends when things became too intimate. This fear was early determined to be related to his incestuous feelings toward his sister. In fact, a preponderant number of his girl friends even had the same name. His main attitude to these girls is a desire to show them off, and he (like his parents) is very conscious of their background (financial, religious, etc.) as well as their appearance (essentially chosen on narcissistic principles). There is also a great deal of latent passive homosexuality, with a history of one fellatio experience during his college years. Since beginning his analysis such fears have come up quite frequently and seem to have a great deal to do with his having begun his first consistent affair.

His past history is one of relative success in school, college, the Marine Corps, and business. There is a highly ambivalent attitude toward his bosses, teachers, etc., with competition and at the same time a strong desire to please, but to date there has been no evidence to show any provocative or masochistic behavior.

There were, however, memories of beating fantasies recovered from early childhood. From certain associations, it was suggested to him that bed-wetting must have played an important role in his life. He confirmed this and went on to talk about secrets. These secrets had to do with masturbation, which was forgotten as such. What was remembered were screen memories having to do with things which had to be hidden from father. Around the age of four or five, he stole a lead soldier from a store, since father would allow nothing military in the house, and hid it in the attic until night. After going to bed, he would get his soldier and take it to bed with him.

He later remembered something else he hid in the attic. This was a kerchief (a red one) and a piece of rope. When going to bed, he would put the kerchief on like a "loincloth" and wind the rope around his body. Masturbation could not be recalled. This memory was associated with his first going to Sunday School and learning about Moses and the Egyptian Pharaoh, and how badly the Jewish slaves were treated in Egypt.

Further associations led to memories of playing a game with a friend which they called Pharaoh and the Slave. Both preferred being the slave. Whether actual beating took place is still uncertain, but in his words, one "pretended to beat the other" (ten years old).

Later (adolescent) masturbation fantasies which were remembered always had a great deal of oral content. There were ideas of having fellatio performed on him, and also ideas of his performing fellatio upon himself, the latter being the more frequent fantasy. He remembers his first nocturnal emission: he dreamed of a close friend of his sister's who was rather large-breasted. He sees her walking toward him in the street with her breasts uncovered. He has an emission and awakens.

Discussion

Kris opened the discussion by pointing out the difference between the beating fantasy in its manifest form as outlined by Freud (1919) in his original paper on this subject, and the nature of the clinical material presented here. All of the cases reported had beating fantasies as an integral part of the clinical material, yet the form in which these were obtained varied from instances of overt perversions, through neurotic behavior, to character neuroses. This contrasted with the original observations made by Freud in a limited number of cases in which the fantasy was obtained in a relatively pure form and could be analyzed back through its stages of development, one stage of which was an unconscious fantasy in which the person himself was being beaten. In Freud's cases, these fantasies were always associated with masturbatory activity and existed or were recovered in the analysis as masturbatory fantasies. In the clinical material presented for consideration, for example Case 2, the beating fantasy is an integral part of the masturbatory practice of the adult and is acted out in a perverse manner as part of the gratification of the masturbatory act. Yet, in this case, not only is the fantasy acted out in the form of self-inflicted beating of the buttocks in order to produce an erection, but the fantasy is also different than the ones described by Freud in that the fantasy is of the individual himself being beaten by a woman as part of the masturbatory fantasy. In Case 3, the beating fantasy is more like that described by Freud in which a man is beating a son on the covered buttocks. But this fantasy also plays a role in part of the adult patient's perverse sexual activity, which includes fetishistic acts.

These comments led to the fact that the overt form of the beating fantasy as presented by a patient, whether in the course of neurotic or of perverse behavior, is not all there is to the fantasy. Rather, it was felt that, like a dream, the fantasy has both a manifest and latent content. The manifest content can, to use the analogy from the dream, assume a variety of forms, from the one described first by Freud of someone being beaten by an authority figure, to the more direct one, as in Case 3, of a father beating the son, or, to the form of the fantasy of the individual himself being beaten, by a woman in this case.

However, it was recognized that behind such a conscious fantasy there is a latent content, a latent meaning, which varies from one person to the other, depending upon the earlier genetic experiences of the particular individual. Thus, in Case 5, an adult woman whose analysis was complete, it was possible to trace the manifest form of the masturbatory beating fantasy in which she was "observing a woman trussed, bound, and face down, buttocks exposed, being beaten and/or raped by an unidentified man. Frequently this man would invite a younger man to view or to participate. Pain played *no* part in the fantasy; the patient was always an onlooker." This manifest form of the fantasy changed in the course of the analysis and she found herself identified with the second man. In the course of the analysis it was possible to uncover the latent content of such a beating fantasy, and the clinical material showed that the fantasy had many meanings; it was overdetermined. It meant watching mother and father have intercourse; that she was the second man, invited to participate with father in the sexual assault on mother; that in order to be a man she had the desire for the phallus; that she was the child invited to participate with the parents in their sexual activity; that she was the victim (mother) having intercourse with father; that, bound and helpless, she was not accountable to her superego for her oedipal wishes; and that the anal regression protected her against castration anxiety. Thus the manifest form of the fantasy contained elements which provided for gratification of voyeuristic tendencies as well as a bisexual identification with a male and a female figure in primal scene fantasies. There were, in addition, defenses against superego condemnations of such fantasies and a defense against castration anxiety by means of regression.

It was pointed out, incidentally, in connection with Case 5 as well as Case 6, that the changing form of the beating fantasy was similar to that reported by Anna Freud (1923) where she traced the vicissitudes of a conscious masturbatory fantasy to its ultimate sublimation and seeming extinction via an attempt at creative literary work.

A statement made by Anna Freud in this article caused considerable discussion. The statement which sparked this discussion is: "The pleasure derived from the fantasy was more and more confined to the climax itself, which was preceded as well as followed by 'pain.' " The discussion centered around several questions. The first was concerned directly with the fantasy itself: whether pain was considered part of the fantasy. In Case 5, for example, pain was no part of the fantasy itself, in either its original or later form. In contrast, in Case 6, pain was an integral part of the initial form of the fantasy, the patient's fantasy being "hanging by my thumbs, stretched from head to toe, beaten but never killed—to the point of unbearable pain—but not enough to kill." However, as the fantasy changed its form, the factor of pain disappeared from the manifest form of the fantasy. In Case 2 pain was also an integral part of the fantasy itself, including not only the beating as a painful act but the addition of water to make it hurt more and hence be more exciting. In contrast, in Case 3, pain does not appear as an integral part of the fantasy. The discussion centered about the question of whether pain need be an integral part of a beating fantasy or whether it may be implied in the nature of the beating act itself. Certainly the clinical material in these instances seemed to be equally divided, as was the opinion and experience of the members of the group who entered into the discussion.

Arising out of this discussion came the larger question of the role of pain in relation to the sexual excitement of beating fantasies and practices. The clinical material suggests that in the perverse activities, as outlined in Cases 2 and 3, pain was an integral part of the masturbatory activity. From this arose the question as to whether pain becomes the source of pleasure and excitement in these activities or whether it is a necessary precondition for the gratification that the patient experiences. This last question is related to the much larger question of the role of pain in masochistic individuals, as to whether the pain becomes only a necessary precondition for some gratification, paying the piper before the dance, as it were, or whether the pain in and of itself assumes a pleasurable quality. By means of the pain, superego demands have been met and gratified. The panel, which had originally raised the question of the role of pain in the sexual excitement of beating fantasies, felt that they had no specific data or answers to this question. The clinical experience of the members of the Group proved equally inconclusive. As was pointed out, this has been a moot point in analytic literature since the problem of masochism began to be discussed.

The attention of the Group then turned toward Case 4, in which the problem was somewhat different from that brought up in the previous clinical material. In this case, that of a young man in his middle twenties, there is no history of a conscious beating fantasy that had been recovered. Rather, the problem is one of a masochistic character neurosis in which the patient's object relationships reproduce an unconscious beating fantasy. Masturbation had not occurred consciously. There were, however, memories of times of excitement, pleasure, and guilt at seeing father beat a household pet or at punishments which the patient was instrumental in bringing down upon a younger brother. In his relationship with men and women he would create situations in which someone close to him was exposed to the wrath of some authority figure. This could be traced back to being a repetition of the early family situation. In connection with this case, the question arose, not only of the nature of the beating fantasy that was being lived out via the character neurosis (this is similar to the cases described by Anna Freud in 1948), but also of the role of identification with a long-suffering sadomasochistic father. The father in this particular case, while being passive and yielding in most of his relationships, would, on occasion, such as the times he beat the dog, give vent to severely sadistic behavior. The patient, who identified with this male figure as part of the usual resolution of the oedipal phase, thus had an added determinant both to the strength of his beating fantasy and to its being taken up into his character structure. The fantasy seemingly had been dissolved only to reappear as part of his self-representation.

Whether the perpetuation of a beating fantasy in connection with infantile masturbation requires some such additional determinant was considered. The questions had arisen in this connection as to what it is that leads a patient to elaborate a beating fantasy rather than some other type of masochistic fantasy, and what makes for the continuation and influence of such a fantasy in a given patient. In Case 4 it seemed that aside from other experiences of his early life such as frequent enemas, etc., the identification with a sadomasochistic father was an added factor making for the particular type of character structure that developed.

Another question that followed from consideration of this case was the relative importance of oedipal and preoedipal components in beating fantasies. The first problem is of determining whether repressed drive derivatives should be attributed to the oedipal or preoedipal phase. In a given instance, it was felt that it would very often be difficult to determine the relative role and weight of oedipal and preoedipal components. On the one hand, it was felt that perhaps this is the sort of situation where direct observation of children might throw some light on the relative weights of these factors. On the other hand, as was pointed out by Kris, many advances in theoretical knowledge in psychoanalysis have come from work with adult patients. This has come about as a result of the reconstructive work done with an adult patient, suggesting new fields for exploration, later confirmed by direct observation of children.

A sidelight of this discussion was the observation that the phallic mother may often substitute for the figure of the father in the direct form and origin of a beating fantasy. This seemed to have been demonstrated in Case 6, and was suggested by Case 4. This substitution of a phallic mother means that development has proceeded on to the phallic-oedipal stage from the anal-sadistic phase; otherwise the concept of a phallic woman would not emerge. Thus it was felt that beating fantasies represent a regression from the phallic-oedipal level to an anal-sadistic level of libidinal development. Such regression would be determined by the vicissitudes of the oedipal phase as well as by preoedipal factors determining fixation points, such as the frequent enemas given to the patient in Case 4.

The relationship of beating fantasies to a masochistic neurosis and the difficulty of determining the nature of the fantasy behind the manifest symptoms from the symptom complex alone were important questions raised. It was pointed out that beating fantasies are but one of a variety of masochistic fantasies in general. It must not be assumed, therefore, that the basic fantasy of a masochistic disorder is necessarily a beating fantasy. There are many other forms of masochistic fantasy, which may appear similar on superficial examination to the living out of a beating fantasy. As it was originally understood, according to Freud's statement of the subject, the beating fantasy was a masturbatory fantasy having to do with sibling rivalry and with the desire to see the sibling in an unfavorable situation. The punishment the sibling received was gratifying in so far as it satisfied the desire to see the sibling debased in the eyes of the punishing parent. Freud also included, in passing, the statement that the fantasy has its origin in an incestuous attachment to the father.

It must be recognized that the first conscious form of the fantasy also gratifies other impulses, i.e., sadistic impulses toward the rival as well as voyeuristic drives which may be associated with primal scene experiences or fantasies. The transformation of this first form of the fantasy to the second, unconscious version comes about by means of both identification with the debased rival and regression to an anal-sadistic stage of libidinal organization in which being the object of a beating by the parent is equated with being loved by that parent. The masochistic transformation is brought about by the combination of identification and regression. This means that the internal situation must be ripe for such a transformation to occur; the presence of such a fantasy does not lead in and of itself to the masochistic disorder. In turn, the fantasy in this second form then feeds into the masochistic groundwork which already exists, and further adds to it. This means that probably there are masochistic fantasies pre-existing which may then be utilized or which may come to expression via the beating fantasy in its second stage. There are, of course, many other types of masochistic fantasies which are not expressed via a beating fantasy.

The clinical material presented showed essentially two broad groups of patients with beating fantasies. In one group were those with a fantasy which had existed in childhood. In these patients it had undergone transformations and seemingly was no longer operative, at least in the conscious life of the patient, even though it influenced later neurotic behavior. The second broad group were those patients who currently were using conscious beating fantasies in association with their sexual gratification. These were, for example, the patients in Cases 2 and 3, and possibly in Case 4. The question arose: in this last group of patients in whom beating fantasies occurred currently, were these the only form of masochistic gratification shown by these patients? If not, under what conditions would beating fantasies as such make their appearance in contrast to other masochistic fantasies? In Case 3 it was clear that there were many other masochistic fantasies being acted out in the course of the perversion and that the beating fantasy, while occupying an important position was not the only source of the patient's perverse gratification. Based on the clinical material of Cases 2, 3, and 4, it was speculated that such patients might have an upsurge of beating fantasies after they had committed or fantasied some hostile or destructive act. Thus the beating fantasy would, in addition to its many other determinants, represent a form of punishment at the behest of the superego for the fantasied or actual hostile or destructive act. This suggests that superego demands in such patients will, under these conditions, be markedly increased, requiring some additional form of atonement as well as an atonement for other fantasies.

There were many other questions touched upon that were not considered specifically. These questions can be grouped as follows.

1. The relation between beating fantasies and specific events of the patient's history (childhood). Attention was called to this general area (beating fantasies and screen memories), but the majority of the questions under this heading remain to be considered. They are: (a) the significance of physical punishment in childhood; (b) the effect of hostile and, in particular, of guilt-producing parents; (c) the importance of sibling rivalry; (d) the importance of voyeurism and exhibitionism in childhood; and (e) the importance of these factors or of other considerations in determining whether a patient elaborates a beating fantasy as distinct from other kinds of masochistic fantasies.

2. The relationship between beating fantasies and object relations in general. For example, what is the importance in beating

fantasies of the patient's unconscious attitude toward his rival, that is, wishing to see him beaten as against wishing to be beaten in his place? The views of Marie Bonaparte (1953) regarding the role of clitoral passivity in feminine masochism were considered briefly in this regard. In summary these are: (a) *Every girl* passing through the passive oedipus complex—which occurs at the height of the phallic phase, while anal-sadistic erotism is still active—must have unconsciously fantasied being beaten on the clitoris by the father's penis. (b) The fantasy "a child is being beaten" is the psychosexual connecting link by which clitoridal erotism (after being predominantly active and sadistic) evolves into full vaginality by way of a passive, masochistic regression to the original state of infantile phallic passivity. (c) The fate of the active, sadistic oedipus complex in girls hinges on the castration complex. The clitoris, as the executive organ of infantile phallic sadism, becomes depreciated, and the little girl then desires the blows of the father's penis.

3. The influence which beating fantasies may have on the entire course and orientation of a patient's life. Is this significantly related to: (a) whether the fantasy is conscious or unconscious, and/or (b) to whether the fantasy was a conscious concomitant of masturbation in adolescence or adult life? The group felt that the answer would require a detailed clinical investigation which was beyond its scope.

The second session on the beating fantasies was opened with a verbal case report by a member of the Study Group of the treatment of a six-and-one-half-year-old girl whose analysis was begun when she was three and one-half years old. This is a case from the Child Study Center of New Haven and therefore much was known about the child from birth on, as well as about the family relationships. Thus, for example, it was known that the child had never been subject to physical punishment but rather that she had, when necessary, been scolded or admonished. By and large the parents were devoted and attentive, although this had to be qualified by the fact that the child was the oldest of three siblings and hence had had ample opportunity for the development of sibling rivalry as well as other fantasies. This had been observed in many of her relationships in nursery school where she was under observation. The main point of the presentation was the fact that, during the second year of her analysis, the child developed the fantasy that her analyst would hit her in the face three times. This was one form of her oedipal transference feelings, as expressed toward the analyst. This fantasy, which had been expressed approximately a year and a half prior to the current presentation, had not recurred in any form, nor had there been any other expression of the desire for some form of "beating" in the transference. The discussion of this case took into account several features which were not related specifically to beating fantasies, but one aspect of the discussion led back to the questions that had originally been raised and touched on in the previous session.

It was apparent from the knowledge of the family and their relationships that this was a little girl who had not been exposed to physical punishment in the course of her life up to that point. Therefore it was of great interest to see the emergence of a desire to be hit in the face as an expression of her positive transference feelings toward her analyst. This led into the general area of the relationship between beating fantasies and specific events of the patient's childhood. It was apparent in this case that the desire to be hit, to be beaten, seemed to have no direct relationship to specific events of her life. In the cases reported in detail by the panelists, the occurrence of physical beating seemed to have played a minor part in the lives of most of these patients (however, one panelist reported a patient with beating fantasies whose father had spanked her every morning until she stopped wetting her bed at the age of thirteen). This would seem to point to the fact that the absence of physical trauma need not influence nor determine the form of the beating fantasy, and conversely, the presence of severe physical punishment need not play an important role.

It became evident that the occurrence of the beating fantasy is not merely a derivative of external stimulation, but is part of the intrapsychic development. However, the relationship between beating fantasies and guilt feelings due to traumatic experiences or influences in childhood was emphasized. In this connection, such factors as sibling rivalry leading to a desire to see the sibling punished or in some way removed from the scene, with consequent

guilt when reality coincides with the fantasy, can play a large role
in producing the transformation of stages of a beating fantasy.

In relation to the problem of the beating fantasy of the six-and-
a-half-year-old girl who developed the fantasy that her analyst
would hit her in the face, Case 8 assumed new importance. In the
latter, there was no evidence in the adult patient of the presence
of a beating fantasy, either in the nature of perverse activity,
characterologic disturbances, or current masturbatory practices.
However, in the course of his analysis, the patient recovered memories of a beating fantasy from early childhood. The associations
had to do with masturbation, stealing, and the memory of going
to bed and putting a kerchief on, like a "loin-cloth" while wind-
ing a rope around his body. This memory was associated with
Sunday School and learning about Moses, the Egyptian Pharaoh,
and how badly Jewish slaves were treated in Egypt. Further associations then led to the memory of playing games with a friend
which they called "Pharaoh and the Slave." Both preferred being
the slave. It is not certain whether actual beating took place, but
in the patient's words, "one pretended to beat the other." However, later adolescent masturbatory fantasies which were remembered had always had a great deal of oral content. Thus it would
seem from this case that there had been transitory beating fantasies, probably associated with masturbation, which disappeared
and have exerted no appreciable influence in terms of the patient's
later personality. On the other hand, this patient showed a latent
passive homosexual drive which was acted out on one occasion and
which was very strongly defended against in the course of analysis.

Kris observed that there was a common pattern in all of the
cases presented in spite of great variation in symptomatology and
character structure. Regardless of whether the clinical picture was
that of perversion, of masochistic character neurosis, or of symptom
neurosis with masochistic overtones, all of these patients exhibited
strong attachment to the father. It was in relation to the father
that so much of the sadomasochistic behavior occurred. The existence of this common pattern led Kris to suggest that the beating
fantasy represents not only a wish to be loved by the father, as
Freud (1919) had suggested in his original paper, but also a wish
to be loved *sexually* by the father (as part of the normal oedipal

constellation), and that such an infantile wish to be loved sexually by the father was often, perhaps regularly, conceived by the child as being beaten by him. Presumably, this corresponds to the frequent, almost ubiquitous infantile sexual theory that what father does to his sexual partner (i.e., mother) is to beat her. This widespread, sadistic concept of intercourse, he pointed out, shows and is related to the importance of anal as well as of sadomasochistic experiences and impulses in the mind of the child.

Kris pointed up that, if this suggestion is correct, then one would expect that beating fantasies would be almost universal at some time in the life of every patient, just as other fantasies (rescue fantasies, castration fantasies, etc.) are. Viewed in this way, the case presented at the second session and Case 8 would seem to confirm such a hypothesis, for in each of these patients there was found a transitory beating fantasy in childhood which had no later marked effect on development. In contrast, in the other cases presented, beating fantasies occupied an important role in adult life. For these patients, as well as other patients in whom beating fantasies play such an important part, the fantasies represent one form of the infantile wish to be loved sexually by father. To borrow from the analogy of the dream, such a wish represents the latent content of every beating fantasy. Therefore, the manifest content, again in terms of the dream, can vary tremendously in accordance with experiences that are used by the ego to make up the form of the fantasy. The focus of interest then shifts from attempting to understand why beating fantasies occur, to understanding why the almost universal beating fantasies assume such importance in the psychosexual life of particular patients. To continue the analogy of the dream, it becomes equally important to understand the nature of the changes that occur in the transition from the latent to the manifest forms seen later on.

This concept, advanced by Kris, served to clarify a number of obscure questions that had been raised in previous discussions. For example, it had been shown by the clinical cases, as well as by additional examples from the Group, that the presence or absence of physical punishment in childhood seemed to play no apparent role in determining the development of significant beating fantasies. But the actual realities of childhood paled in light of this suggestion, except perhaps as an additional fixating experience when reality coincided with the inner wishes of the child. Thus the question for discussion about beating fantasies returned to why, in particular patients, these fantasies assumed the importance they did, and hence to the broader problem of the development of sadomasochistic personalities. Other questions raised, such as those about identification with a suffering, sadomasochistic father, the role of hostile and guilt-producing parents, the importance of sibling rivalry, and the problem of why a beating fantasy is a particular form of masochistic fantasy, in light of this proposal, could be considered as belonging to the realm of factors that produce a masochistic personality structure and hence strengthen the importance of the ubiquitous beating fantasy.

Stimulated by these suggestions, the attention of the Group then turned to the related question of what particular functions the beating fantasies played in the mental life of a particular patient. Several speakers pointed out that these functions could be expected to vary widely. One member, for instance, reminded the Group that this was equally true of many sexual wishes and actions, e.g., of heterosexual intercourse, or as Anna Freud had shown, of homosexual behavior. In the course of the discussion, a case was reported of an eleven-year-old orphan girl with an abnormal and inadequate ego development, manifested by impulsive, erratic behavior as well as many signs of defects in superego development. This girl had, in the course of therapy, expressed the fantasy that she might have a father who would beat her. This led to the suggestion by others that masochistic fantasies in general, and beating fantasies in particular, might have special value, at least in some fairly disturbed cases, as a way of maintaining or establishing some sort of relationship with the world of objects. This object relationship function of the beating fantasy would then represent a spread to all objects of the original desire to be loved by one particular object, the father, and would be in the service of maintaining some form of object relationship in a desperate effort to maintain contact with the outside world.

In consideration of Case 1, it was proposed that there might be another function to beating fantasies in particular, and perhaps masochistic fantasies in general. This patient, it will be remembered, was a thirty-six-year-old man who indulged in a sadistic perversion which consisted in sex play involving a couple, usually husband and wife. The husband would sit on the floor in the corner of the room while the patient would whip the man's wife. He would not beat hard enough to inflict injury, but just enough to make her cry out in pain. In the back of the patient's mind was always the question, "why did the husband let him get away with it?" This patient also visited prostitutes who would allow him to administer token thrashings. This enabled him to function as a potent male in the sexual act. In the analysis this was related back to a time when he had grown too big for his mother to administer corporal punishment and she would call upon the boarder in their home, a big policeman, to punish him. One time, when he was especially naughty toward his mother, this man gave him a thrashing on the buttocks. He would often provoke the mother, usually by hitting her in the abdomen, even though he knew that mother would call upon the boarder to punish him. It seemed that the sadistic behavior manifested in his perverse activity was a means to a masochistic end. It served as a means of carrying out the unconscious wish to be beaten. It was suggested that this "request" to be beaten may not be desired as an end in and for itself, but is a displacement standing in lieu of a greater danger, i.e., castration. It was questioned whether, in terms of this patient, the beating wish involving the buttocks might not be a sacrifice of the buttocks for the penis. In this way, his oedipal fantasies and desires could be acted out in an aggressive way with mother with immunity from the threat of castration by virtue of the fact that he would be beaten instead. It was felt in the discussion which followed that this suggestion, while plausible, probably applied only to this case. There was not sufficient clinical evidence to warrant such a generalized assumption as to the function of a beating fantasy. It was pointed out once again in this connection that beating fantasies, like many other fantasies, can serve multiple functions, varying from individual to individual. If in a specific case they served such a role as suggested above, it did not mean that this was a universal function of beating fantasies in particular, nor of masochistic fantasies in general.

Consideration turned toward the actual form of the beating

fantasy itself. It was pointed out that several factors seemed to enter into it. Voyeuristic and exhibitionistic drives, based upon real or fantasied primal scene experiences, seemed to play a part both in the visual and auditory content of the fantasy. The role of the hand in determining the auditory aspects was mentioned, which led to a consideration of the following linguistic and etymological observations.

Certain clinical features observed in beating fantasies, such as the mention of having overheard beating of a child in an adjoining room or bathroom, the conspicuous absence of the beating hand in some cases, the sometimes specific use of onomatopoetic wording in the description of actual or fantasied beating events, led to consideration of the problem in acoustic-linguistic-auditory terms, and to examination of whether sound is not one of the prominent features in such cases. The close associations of father and sound (his "roaring" or "thundering" voice, paternal flatus, and other powerful noises) are of course well known to analysts. It may be thought likely that the meaning of paternal "thunder" is considerably heightened under the impact of a punishing or otherwise threatening situation, as exemplified by Zeus the "thunderer," the roaring bull or lion deities, clinical manifestations like brontephobia, etc. Moreover, in surveying the more common terms used to designate the act of beating, it was found that a number of these words are of imitative origin, that is, derived from sounds produced by the beating; etymologically, they are formed on the basis of the onomatopoetic principle, in imitation of sounds actually perceived.[1] To this group belong words like spank, slap, clap, and knock, possibly also sock, slug, and bang (though the last stems from the ancient nordic *banga* = hammer). These words, then, can be viewed as verbal formations based on auditory perceptions of the beating act just as the perceptions of the primal scene, of anal functions, etc., are so frequently and prevalently auditory. In fact, some expressions denoting aggression have a close relation to coital words and vice versa:

In English, to knock or to bang can be used vulgarly as a sexual term, e.g., to "knock up" a woman, impregnate her. An obsolete

---

[1] See Niederland (1958).

meaning of the word "clap" which, incidentally, was also used in the same combination—to "clap up" a woman is to press, cleave, or lie close. Whether the American slang term "clap" for gonorrhea is based on this meaning remains undecided, at least at the time of this writing. However, to knock under (to yield, succumb) and the double meaning of smack (a loud kiss as well as a resounding slap) are worth noting. The knocking up-knocking under situation between the beater and the beaten one repeats in a sense the incubus-succubus position in coitus.

In Italian, *suonare* (*suono* = sound) is used both ways: *una bella suonata* may indicate a good spanking, i.e., *una bella suonata* understood as *una bella bastonata*; but it may also mean, in vulgar language, *una bella fuottata*, i.e., a good "lay." The usual word for beat, *battere* (from Latin, *battuo*), can be used in the same sense, when slightly modified by a preceding "s," e.g., *sbattere una donna* (to "screw" a woman). The modifying "s" here reduces the aggressive meaning of *battere* as, for instance, also the obscene word *fottere* or *fuottere* is transformed into the de-aggressivized verb *sfuottere*. Of some interest also is the Italian slang expression *rompere i coglioni* or *rompere le scatole* which is only addressed by one man to another, usually in an extremely hostile fashion, and literally means "to break the testicles."

The Hebrew word for beat, *hakeh*, is used in the Talmud in various connections. In Tractat Yoma the word is defined as "to strike, to produce sound, to play." Tractat Parah, on the other hand, uses the same word in a discussion of an accidental lesion which causes the breaking of the hymen in a virgin. The Talmud mentions *hakeh* = beat (the hymen) in this context, thus, causing a lesion to it. There is another Hebrew term for spanking, *harbiz*. Its literal meaning is to go down on all fours, like an animal, to receive a beating. The succubus position mentioned above, in the beating as well as the coital procedure, seems to be reflected also in this term, here *more ferarum*.

In Spanish, perhaps the most common beating term is simply *dar* (give) or *dar el palo* (give the stick). This exists also in Italian in the idiomatic expression *dare le botte*. In the combination *da mi lo bene* it is sexually tinged.

In German, the coital word *ficken* has definite aggressive connotations. In old Dutch the same word means beat. An obsolete term for the female genital, in vulgar language, is *Fickmuhle*—literally, "fuck-mill"—which has connotations of "clip-clap" pertaining to the image of a mill. Another beating term, *stossen,* also is a slang word for sexual activity.

Further worth noting is the English expression "a good spanking" and the Italian and French counterparts (respectively): *una bella battuta, une bonne raclée.* The last, which literally refers to a carpenter's planing wood, is rendered *hobeln* in German, a frequently used slang word for coitus comparable to "screw" in American slang.

Without giving further material from clinical and nonclinical observations in this preliminary note, the author of these observations pointed to some of the data presented by the members of the panel: the "thundering noise . . . and primal scene noises" in Case 5, the "knocked down" fantasy of the patient described in Case 6, the references to "thunderstorm" in Case 4 and "groaning and moaning" in Case 2, and the role of sound in the beating fantasies and activities of the patient in Case 3. Additional clinical data seem to lend support to these findings and to amplify certain aspects, pertaining mainly to the connection—via sound—of primal scene and beating fantasies. The fact that both the sounds as well as the movements producing them are *rhythmical* provides another linkage.

With respect to the idea so commonly found in beating fantasies that the person being beaten is tied up, the suggestion was made by Kris that it might be related to tightening of the muscles of the thigh and buttocks by the child in crural masturbation, or in retaining feces. Thus, in the fantasy, being held tightly would represent the unconscious idea of "holding tight" in these pleasurable and exciting situations. This suggestion is related to Kris's observation of the importance of anal experiences and impulses in the origin of beating fantasies.

In his concluding summary, Kris remarked that it appeared to him that the chief question which was still unanswered, of those which had occupied the attention of the group, was that of the difference between beating fantasies of the type Freud reported on the one hand and, on the other hand, those associated with or expressed in overt perverse behavior.

It might be noted that many other questions were raised but were not answered. For example, the very important question raised originally:"what determines the degree to which beating fantasies permeate or influence a patient's whole life?" is part of the larger problem of the mutual interrelationship between fantasy and development in general, and of its importance in masochistic development in particular. Another question raised, as to the contribution of each of the various stages of psychosexual development to the dynamics and genesis of beating fantasies, was touched upon and suggestions were made for future investigation and theoretical formulation. However, the details of such contributions on the different levels of development still remain to be worked out. One aspect of the relationship between beating fantasies and object relations in general was considered partially, that is, that beating fantasies in certain patients with defective ego development serve the function of maintaining an object relationship. But other aspects of the relationship between beating fantasies and object relations remain to be worked out in greater detail. For instance, a specific question in this area has to do with the importance in beating fantasies of the patient's unconscious attitudes toward his rival—wishing to see him beaten versus wishing to be beaten in his place. The topic of feminine masochism, both what it is and its relation to beating fantasies, was only briefly touched upon. Marie Bonaparte's view on the role of clitoral passivity in feminine masochism touched on this area, but detailed consideration of this very important relationship was not forthcoming. Other questions that related to the importance, if any, of whether the fantasy was conscious or unconscious, or whether it was a conscious concomitant of masturbation in adolescence or adult life or was only conscious in childhood, also remain to be studied in greater detail. The latter questions relate not only to the problems of beating fantasies specifically, but to the still unsolved problems of the role and importance of fantasy in characterologic development in general, and belong in the realm of further investigation.

Summary

Specific contributions were made in terms of the problems regarding beating fantasies and their role in the mental life of patients. Ernst Kris suggested that beating fantasies represent a form of the infantile desire to be loved sexually by father and, as such, are perhaps universal in their occurrence. This thought seemed valuable in considering the role of beating fantasies in mental life and opened the larger question: What determines the development of a masochistic character or neurosis, whether or not the beating fantasy is used in the service of the masochistic tendencies? Other contributions made concerned some factors relating to the genesis, function, and actual form of beating fantasies, as well as to the part played by noise and sound in such fantasies.

BIBLIOGRAPHY

Aarons, Z. A. (1959), A Study of a Perversion and an Attendant Character Disorder. *Psychoanal. Quart.*, 28:481-492.*

Bergler, E. (1938), Preliminary Phases of the Masculine Beating Fantasy. *Psychoanal. Quart.*, 7:514-536.

—— (1948), Further Studies on Beating Fantasies. *Psychiat. Quart.*, 22:480-486.

—— (1956), Further Studies in Depersonalization. *Psychoanal. Quart.*, 24:268-277.

Bonaparte, M. (1953), *Female Sexuality*. New York: International Universities Press, pp. 83-97.

Feldman, S. S. (1959), Anxiety and Orgasm. *Psychoanal. Quart.*, 20:528-549.*

Freud, A. (1923), The Relation of Beating Fantasies to a Day Dream. *Int. J. Psychoanal.*, 4:89-102.

—— (1948), Certain Types of Stages of Social Maladjustment. In *Searchlights on Delinquency*, ed. K. R. Eissler. New York: International Universities Press, pp. 193-204.

Freud, S. (1918), From the History of an Infantile Neurosis. *Standard Edition*, 17:46-47, 1955.

—— (1919), A Child Is Being Beaten. *Standard Edition*, 17:175-204, 1955.

—— (1924), The Economic Principle of Masochism. *Standard Edition*, 19:165-169, 1961.

—— (1925), Some Physiological Consequences of the Anatomical Distinction between the Sexes. *Standard Edition*, 19:245-254, 1961.

Hendrick, I. (1933), Pregenital Anxiety in a Passive-Feminine Character. *Psychoanal. Quart.*, 2:68-93.

Johnson, L. B. T. (1939), A Woman Is Being Beaten: an Analytic Fragment. *Psychoanal. Rev.*, 17:259-267.

Lester, M. (1957), The Analysis of an Unconscious Beating Fantasy in a Woman. *Int. J. Psychoanal.*, 38:22-31.

Loewenstein, R. M. (1957), A Contribution to the Psychoanalytic Theory of Masochism. *J. Amer. Psychoanal. Assn.*, 5:197-234.*

* This contribution was made after the panel held its meetings.

Niederland, W. (1958), Linguistic Observations on Beating Fantasies, *J. Hillside Hosp.*, 7:202-207, 1958.*

Rascovsky, L. (1945), Aportación al Estudio de las Fantasias de Flagelación (Contribution to the Study of Flagellation Fantasies). *Rev. Psicoanal. Buenos Aires*, 3:19-42.

Schmiedeberg, M. (1948), On Fantasies of Being Beaten. *Psychoanal. Rev.*, 35:303-308.

Singer, M. (1960), Borderline Case Fantasies. *The Psychoanalytic Study of the Child*, 15:310-356. New York: International Universities Press.*

——— (1958a), Beating Fantasies, Auditory Hallucinations and Primal Scene. *The Psychoanalytic Study of the Child*, 13:471-503. New York: International Universities Press.*

* This contribution was made after the panel held its meetings.

Regressive Ego Phenomena in Psychoanalysis

EDWARD D. JOSEPH, M.D., *Reporter*

Participants: Herbert Aldendorff, M.D.—Leon L. Altman, M.D.—
Jacob A. Arlow, M.D.—Stuart Asch, M.D.—David Beres, M.D.—
Charles Brenner, M.D.—Bernard Brodsky, M.D.—Kenneth T. Calder,
M.D.—John Donadeo, M.D.—Ellis Feer, M.D.—Bernard D. Fine, M.D.
—Jules Glenn, M.D.—Merl Jackel, M.D.—Edward D. Joseph, M.D.
—Arnold Kallen, M.D.—William P. Kapuler, M.D.—Louis Kaywin,
M.D.—Edward Kloth, M.D.—Mathew Levine, M.D.—Leo S. Loomie,
Jr., M.D.—Betty Magruder, M.D.—Ernest Marcus, M.D.—John B.
McDevitt, M.D.—Burness E. Moore, M.D.—Werner Nathan, M.D.—
William G. Niederland, M.D.—Eugene Nininger, M.D.—Joshua M.
Perman, M.D.—Arnold Z. Pfeffer, M.D.—David L. Rubinfine, M.D.—
Oscar Sachs, M.D.—Howard Scal, M.D.—Howard H. Schlossman, M.D.
—Jay Schorr, M.D.—Irwin Solomon, M.D.—Rebecca G. Solomon, M.D
—Jacob E. Stump, M.D.—Herbert F. Waldhorn, M.D.—Martin Wangh,
M.D.—Philip Weissman, M.D.—George H. Wiedeman, M.D.

IN TERMS OF MODERN structural theory,[1] the structure of the mental apparatus is defined in part by the various functions subsumed under the three structures postulated. There has been a trend to

[1] Dr. Jacob A. Arlow, acting as Chairman of the Kris Study Group, outlined the propositions under consideration and reviewed briefly the psychoanalytic concepts involved.

a sharper definition of specific psychic functions, particularly of those included under the functions of the ego. This is in accord with, and grew out of, the concept of the ego which evolved in Freud's writings. In 1923, Freud stated there is "a coherent organization of mental processes which we call the ego. This ego includes consciousness and it controls the approaches to motility, i.e., to the discharge of excitations into the external world; it is this institution in the mind which regulates all its constituent processes, and which goes to sleep at night, though even then it continues to exercise a censorship upon dreams." The recognition of an ego defined by its functions has paved the way for much fruitful research in the past three decades of psychoanalytic thinking. Later studies in this direction have been done by Hartmann, Kris, and Loewenstein (1949), who speak in terms of the mediating function of the ego. The ego is described as "a substructure of personality defined by its functions" (Hartmann, 1950).

The three structures of the mental apparatus arise out of an early undifferentiated psychic state (Hartmann, 1950) and develop into the differentiated structures seen in the fully mature mental apparatus—id, ego, and superego. According to Hartmann (1958) the ego develops partly out of conflict with instinctual drives and reality demands, and partly out of autonomous, conflict-free growth. The growing psychic apparatus is influenced to varying degrees by combinations of inherent maturational forces, learning experiences, and environmental cultural factors. The development of the ego can be described in terms of the development of its separate functions, each of which goes through a progressive process of development and maturation, and each of which may also manifest regressive developments, either normal or pathological. Certain functions pursue an autonomous, conflict-free development, while others develop out of conflict and later attain a secondary autonomy in the mature ego. What is seen in the course of analysis of an adult is the result of such development of both primarily and secondarily autonomous ego functions, as well as manifestations of functions which are involved in conflict.

It is the purpose of the Study Group to examine certain phenomena which manifest themselves during the analytic situation and which represent relatively transient, regressive ego phenomena indicating disturbances in various normally autonomous ego functions. The clinical material to be presented and discussed involves certain ego functions which ordinarily, in nonpsychotic individuals, do not show disturbance. The presentation of the clinical material by the members of the Group allows for examination of the situations under which such disturbances occur in an attempt to ascertain their nature, the forces involved, and the adaptive purposes of such phenomena. In addition, the clinical material illustrates the nature of the structure of the ego and tests its working definition of representing a series of interdependent and interrelated functions.

The comments made in the course of the discussion may be grouped under two main categories: (1) discussion of the clinical material presented by the panel, and (2) theoretical considerations which arose from the clinical material.[2]

Case 1

The patient is a twenty-nine-year-old, married woman in her sixth month of analysis. She had two years of analysis (interrupted for external reasons) with another analyst seven years previously. She came for analysis the second time because she suspected her disappointment in her job and husband stemmed from her own emotional problems.

Her husband is not as successful in work, not as educated, talented, or impressive as she would like. Her job disappoints her because others doing similar work are more successful than she. In general, she is envious, competitive, complaining. She feels she would enjoy intercourse more if her husband mistreated her. Her only sibling is a brother, three years younger. As children, the patient and her brother wore matching clothes for many years. There is much about her appearance today which is masculine. Visual experiences, such as movies or art, are most gratifying to her. Until her menarche, she shared a bathroom with her parents and brother and saw them naked many times; her mother prohibited this sharing after her menarche. The parents had many arguments during which her father would

[2] It should be noted that the clinical material was submitted by a panel which met with Dr. Arlow in advance of the group session. The cases were derived from the panel members' individual practices.

lock himself in a room; the mother would then beat on the door until he let her in.

On seven or eight occasions during her analysis, she has lapsed into a state where her thoughts approximate visual experiences. In a trance-like state, she then describes what she "sees" in her thoughts. She does not believe what she sees is really there, but the vividness of what is seen is much greater than usual. When describing these experiences, the patient moves less on the couch and seems fascinated with her thoughts. Most, if not all, of these thoughts have occurred when she was feeling envy. Often, they involved something being bent, broken, injured or killed. At least five of the visions concerned a sheet, mask, or other piece of cloth covering either a face, a hairy animal like a dog, or "internal organs like bowels." The visions are usually frightening. On two occasions they have been followed by headaches around the eyes. She also had these visions in her first analysis. During her present analysis, she has twice reported seeing similar visions before falling asleep.

In the third hour of analysis, the patient complained of not feeling things deeply enough. Her husband also doesn't have deep enough feelings. Years ago, her mother noted that she, the mother, was over-powered by sex attraction to the father. They had no intercourse before marriage, but the father brought her to a climax without inter-course; he said the mother was terrible to make him do that. "Now I see a man's penis combined with a bowel movement, and they are pushing forward." Then she recalled putting her hand on their chauf-feur's lap at the age of eight and being embarrassed to touch his penis. "Now I see an upright couch with a man standing behind it and pushing it to the ground." She doesn't want to relate herself to the analyst. She cried when G. (an admired boy friend) left her. He once put his mouth on her genitals; she later cooked dinner for him and was upset when he became "sick at his stomach."

In the fourth hour, the patient noted that her mother pushed her father around. She once heard the cook throwing up and was almost sexually aroused. Her mother is a social climber and is upset that the patient is not. The patient's first intercourse was with a merchant marine sailor. "Now I see someone breaking through a wall or a fence." When she was six, some neighbor boys inspected her and the girl next door. "The breaking through the fence is by a vehicle now rather than a human. Now a stick or tree with balls on the end of the branches and small wheels. Now there are people or animals in a cart leaning way back like on a scooter; and one dog chases another beneath the scooter." A nursery rhyme came to her mind, "All I can see is her toes and her hair." She thought of a book where a girl and her mother made a mess of eggs for the father.

A few weeks later, she reported that she could not fall asleep the night before until she thought of a black ball and chain. She felt angry that friends did better than she. She had a dream of mutilated children with one girl having soap suds on her face. The mutilation reminded her of an auto accident her parents and she had shortly before her brother was born. "Now I see a man looking into a hood and coming up dirty and then turning into an ugly creature with a black cloak . . . he looks like a mole . . . and now a man with a handkerchief over his face looking like a bandit and shooting guns or electric currents." She thought of the sensation of getting a shock from an electric socket. She was not hurt in the auto accident, yet she now thought of being hurt around the vagina as if kicked there. The electricity probably relates to her brother and herself having a toy phone that extended from his bedroom, through the bathroom, to her bedroom. Perhaps the soap suds also refer to the bathroom.

In her analysis, this patient frequently uses a partial ego regression as a mechanism of defense. When her ego becomes aware of the emergence of forbidden impulses, it regresses in the form of considering inner thoughts as being from the outside, i.e., reality testing is temporarily and incompletely suspended to the extent that a thought approximates a percept. The patient's reality testing in other areas is adequate; she is not believed to be psychotic. It is possible that the patient uses this particular defense, among other reasons, because of her past history of early, repeated and intense visual trauma. Her defense mechanism would then serve several functions: (1) She is not responsible for her thoughts; she merely sees something. (2) She again has the pleasure of looking at something. (3) By repeating the traumatic experiences in the diluted form of a vision she might overcome her anxiety about them. (4) Perhaps the original visual experiences, like this one, were only thoughts.

Case 2

The patient experienced the Isakower phenomenon (Isakower, 1938) six times during her second year of analysis, during the time that she was pregnant. The first three of these experiences are described below.

The patient was brought up by a weak, alcoholic father and a mother who was subservient to an aunt who supplied the money for the patient's upbringing and education. This aunt was very much a part of the household as the patient was growing up. After the patient had been in analysis for about a year, as a prim young spinster, she became pregnant out of wedlock and married the father of the child. Her new family situation was similar to her original one. Her husband is a student whose wealthy mother gives them money as the aunt had done for the patient's family when she was small. Pregnancy was full-term. The first episode to be described occurred when she was about six months pregnant. Prior to this session, the patient had been talking of how greedy she was. She wanted to rob her aunt, get her money, eat a lot. She felt insatiable and angered by deprivation.

The patient complained that, as a child, she could not reach either parent. Her father played golf or drank; her mother was with the aunt. She wanted to cause the aunt unhappiness. When she had an affair some years ago, her aunt's punishment was to deprive her of listening to music. She liked Bach, whose music "flows." As she talked of this, she had an experience she had had between the ages of six and eight, possibly when asleep. It was as if she were in wax, especially her legs, as if the wax flowed into her mouth. There was no visual or auditory hallucinatory experience. When the analyst asked whether there was difficulty distinguishing inside and outside of her, she said, "Maybe." She felt as though she were sinking into the wax.

After that session, the patient was depressed for a few days. In the next session, she told of wanting to be a good mother but not knowing how. Children have to experience getting all. She wants immediate satisfaction. She enjoys art. When she was a child, music calmed her if she was not picked up. She used to suck and hold a cloth at night. Now she notices herself holding a washcloth or tissue. It has to do with oral satisfaction. The patient's husband sucks her breasts.

The second experience occurred nineteen days later. Prior to it, she continued to talk of her greed. She needed to be protected from and punished for greediness. She feared death during delivery and worried how the baby would get out. Her aunt protected her from her father when he was drunk. The patient gave several examples of being punished by women for pleasant activities in childhood: talking; her interest in her father; masturbation; reading medical books at six or seven. Her father shouted at her for drawing a man with a penis, a picture of her father. She became anxious, wanted to be a good mother, not hurt her baby. The analyst asked whether she feared punishment because of a fear of hurting her baby, or whether just having the baby was a crime. She then described a childhood masturbation fantasy: "I am a nun and restrained. A sensuous man rapes me. Near the orgasm I give up restraint, am liberated and have an orgasm [restraint here refers to an inner restraint]."

As she told this she developed a feeling like the one described above. Her mouth felt dry, and the tongue and roof of her mouth felt swollen. Her body got big. Her hands swelled, especially her left hand, and particularly the fingers which were in contact with the couch. She felt fused with the couch. It was a pleasurable and warm feeling. When asked what it reminded her of, she said, "Swollen breasts and vagina." Most of her body felt swollen and she mentioned parts of the body. The analyst pointed out that she omitted one part of the body, and she said her clitoris did not swell. "This is a terrible thing to think of." This was interpreted by the analyst as a denial of sexual excitement by the fantasy: her clitoris doesn't swell but her body does, and she becomes a baby at the breast. She then said that the clitoris should be ignored and not be there.

The third session to be described was about five weeks later. After complaining that the analyst gave her no advice about her baby, she said a friend had advised her to have a maid for two weeks after the baby was born. Then she felt the baby "flop over." Suddenly she started to hallucinate (her word). She felt swollen all over: mouth, tongue, legs, arms. She felt as if she were sinking into the couch. Her legs felt hollow but heavy. She couldn't get out of the door. She was regressing, becoming a baby, "... doing something to avoid responsibility for the baby. I don't want to be pregnant and want to think of myself as a baby.... I'm heavy, sort of surrounded, in the womb again." She went on to chide the analyst for not giving advice. She needed authorities. She was a slave to the baby, did not want a schedule, did not wish to be drained by the baby. She could do it. She fed her husband and he became fat. She was not weak.

Several childhood experiences and current conflicts influenced the production of these phenomena. For the first month of her life, the patient was given a very dilute formula and therefore cried a great deal. She gained little or no weight, perhaps lost weight, until a new pediatrician changed the formula. The patient was toilet-trained by a strict grandmother who was very clean. She was given enemas. Even now she often holds back her bowel movement for ten or fifteen minutes after she first has the desire to defecate. She finds that there is something pleasant about this.

Case 3

The following incidents were reported in the course of the analysis of a thirty-three-year-old man who is one of identical twins. The first occurred early in his analysis, at a time when he was becoming aware of his close attachment to his twin brother. The patient reported that, while waiting for a bus, he began to look in a store window where he could see his own reflection in the glass. As he looked, he became uncertain whether this was his face and body or that of his twin brother. Then he became sure that it was the twin brother's reflection he was seeing. Suddenly, the reflection changed and it was no longer that of a man, but that of a woman who looked exactly like him, except for having long hair and a womanly figure. Then he became convinced that it was his own image he was seeing, and was frightened.

The second incident was reported at the beginning of the second year of his analysis when, as the result of the analytic work, he was able to move out of the apartment he had shared with his brother and, for the first time in his life, began living by himself. He was both disturbed by this separation and somewhat elated at the progress made. He was fearful of what would become of him since he felt that the separation would result in the death of one or the other twin. Shortly after the move, he placed mirrors so that he could lie in bed and still see himself. He would then *fantasy* that as he looked, he was seeing not himself but the image of his brother, and hence he really was not alone. Simultaneously, he began to eat a great deal and *felt* that his abdomen, which had been flat, was becoming rounded. Often, on the couch, he would pat his stomach and say how full, round, and big it had become, although there had been no outward change in the appearance or size of his abdomen. As it eventually turned out, this was a fantasy of incorporation: the brother existed safely inside of him. It was also a fulfillment of another fantasy that all single people had at a very early time in their lives incorporated a twin brother. While relating all this, on the couch, there were intense biting and chewing movements of his jaws.

The third incident occurred during the course of his wife's pregnancy. About the fifth month of the pregnancy, he reported that, while playing tennis the preceding day, he had suddenly stopped in mid-court and thought to himself, "How can I run with this heavy thing hanging in front of me?" As he thought this, he patted his abdomen and said to himself, "It's so big, it's so large, it gets in my way when I play tennis." Toward the end of his wife's pregnancy, he complained about the tightness of his belt and trousers, saying that they impeded the circulation in his large belly. On occasion, he would loosen his zipper so that there would be a little more room for the enlarged pendulous abdomen that he felt he was carrying. He worried how he could deliver such a large baby and had many fantasies of anal birth.

Of this patient's many problems, an important one is his failure to establish himself completely as a separate individual. He did, and to some extent still does, regard himself as an incomplete person who is complete only in the presence of his twin brother or a substitute. In his relations, he identifies with others, thus completing the unity that he must have. This has occurred everywhere, including the transference, so that when his wife was pregnant, he too felt pregnant. This fantasy points up another aspect of his personality in that he has a marked feminine identification and, as a consequence, has many fantasies of himself as a woman. This is especially true in relation to his twin, for he thinks of himself as the feminine partner. This is lived out in his false perception of the mirror image related in the first incident, i.e., an id wish intruded into an autonomous ego function, perception.

He has a great desire to take in the whole world; his introjective tendencies occur through both eyes and mouth. Combined with this is a destructive drive against which he defends himself constantly. Thus, in the second incident described above, all that became clear at the moment of analysis was his desire to incorporate and save the brother. Only a little later was it possible to show him that the introjective fantasy included one of destroying his brother, an aspect which had been denied, yet which was acted out by his chewing activity as he related these thoughts. Thus his fantasy contained both the destruction of the brother and the assurance that it really was not so, since the brother now safely existed inside him.

One of the remarkable features of this patient is the use of his body to illustrate and live out his associations. For example, in describing his feelings of being a woman, he would cup his hands over his chest as though he actually possessed adult female breasts (there had been transvestite activities in adolescence). He is never sure what type of genital he possesses and often has either to touch or look to see. Much of this is related to a failure to develop a complete body image of himself, for he has always had a mirror image before his eyes. Thus he never knew where he and his brother began

or ended. Equally, he never was sure whether what he saw and felt
was really his or his image's, or the projected image of his feminine
self-representation.

There have been many other evidences of disturbance of reality
testing in addition to those mentioned here. Also, there have been
transient paranoid and hypomanic reactions as well as periods of
depersonalization. However, this patient is classified diagnostically as
borderline rather than psychotic.

Case 4

A leading feature of a panic state in a twenty-year-old, single, Jewish, male writer was a disturbance of the sense of time. The recent
past was experienced as if "compressed." He could not tell, in an emotional way, whether he had met someone yesterday, last week, or three
months ago. The affective tone of remembered experiences lacked the
paling which usually occurs as events slip into the past, and most
things had the vividness of the near present. The symptom was ego-
alien; intellectually he retained awareness of the progression of days,
but emotionally he could not keep the feel of time perspective. Cou-
pled with this was a distortion of the sense of anticipation. He felt
unable to imagine the prospective succession of time intervals—"time
had stopped." Related to these difficulties were an intense dread that
a moving train would not stop, a fear of high places, and an eye sensation the patient called "in-traction, as if I had gone into a mental
crouch."

The onset of the panic which became a chronic pan-anxiety occurred when this patient was watching a boring movie, to kill time,
before taking his current girl friend to his dentist father for emergency treatment.

The patient had suffered a series of narcissistic injuries in adolescence. His first girl friend, so idealized as to be unapproachable physically, was lost to a rival. The next girl, at college, similarly remote,
was again lost to a classmate. Because of this he left school to wander
over the country as a migrant worker. He developed a physical sexual
agility while remaining deeply lonely. When he returned to college,
he took up with a promiscuous girl whose hardness he diagnosed as a
cover for her loneliness. While exercising his own "picaresque" attitude in a number of casual sexual episodes, he strove mainly to bring
this girl to focus her interest on him. He was hurt repeatedly by her
obvious affairs with wealthier boys. Finally, after college, the rebuffs

forced him to give her up. At about this time, he was examined for military service and rejected as unfit by the Army psychiatrist. While he dreaded fighting in Korea, his self-esteem was grossly insulted. Two jobs were attempted; he was fired from both for unrealistic attitudes.

Winning a magazine short-story contest with a prize of $1000 led him to stake all on what he felt to be a desperate gamble. He moved away from home, rented an apartment, began living with a girl whom he had picked up, and who had his mother's maiden name. He tried to write the novel which was to bring him wealth and fame. Failure in writing would necessitate a return to the parental home and acknowledgment that his father's disapproval had been justified. He found this girl friend warm and giving. She went to work to supplement their funds and was physically passionate. But he could not write; no plot seemed significant enough. There was a steady erosion of savings without prospect of replacement. Nor could he tolerate sex. He was afraid that bed noises would make the people next door angry. More dreaded was the loss of his own identity, the merging into the girl friend: "I could not tell where she stopped and I began." He felt like plunging a knife into her when so affected. The panic happened after four months of struggling ineffectively to win the gamble.

His father was a professionally successful, but chronically ill man, bitter in prevailing spirit, an inveterate gambler, harsh and loud in his frequent fights with his wife. She was the daughter of a local politician, thought to be wealthy, who on marriage was discovered to have successfully concealed her family's relative poverty. An extremely patient, wistful person with little drive or taste, she was ever ready to perform humiliating services. The patient had one sibling, a six-year-older brother. The patient, an unwanted child, was born just after the father had lost heavily in the stock-market crash of 1929. He sucked his fingers with satisfaction, shame, and pride of concealment until he was fourteen. There were, successively, two nursemaids, both loved and both stormily dismissed for sexual promiscuity before he was five years of age. He could remember trying to stab one in jealousy when he saw her kissing a boy friend. His childhood neurosis included listening to the sound of his parents' breathing at night to make sure they were not dead. He would have to use the bathroom repeatedly at night, each time with the compulsion of banging the door four or five times. He had a screen memory of intense terror of a buzzing insect while he was in his crib.

There were many memories of his brother who could both be kind to him and beat him up. Deceived at the purpose of a visit to the doctor, he was dragged panic-stricken from a bathroom refuge to the operating table for a tonsillectomy at the age of six. For a time, in treatment, he doubted the reality of a memory of seeing a woman hurtle against the sidewalk from an upper story as he looked from his second-floor window. His parents confirmed he had seen the suicide when he was seven or eight. He was shocked at his father's urging him to lie in support of a lawsuit against a landlord over his falling in the hall when he was about nine. His father was admired for his power, feared for his violent temper, sought after for his admiration of the son's precocity, hated for actually abusing the mother, worried over for his gastric hemorrhages, and belittled for his hypocrisy. The patient was partly schooled for a Bar Mitzvah which was celebrated though depreciated.

As a boy, the patient would pull down the shades lest poor neighbors see the good food they were eating. He lived in daily terror of his rough playmates, fought only once when literally thrown against another youngster by his brother. His adjustment was through manipulating others into new games, e.g., tag in a dark basement. Other boys' aggressiveness and interest in sex sickened him. In college, when he deeply admired an English professor, he could not take the professor's course for credit, but only as an auditor who informally submitted themes. Thus success could be personally scored and the prospect of failure was prediscounted.

In his present illness, the feeling that "time has stopped" defended against his fear of failure by denying that he would be twenty-one and reach manhood when life really counted. Retrospectively, also, time had not run out; the gamble that he could write successfully had not been lost; it was not true that he was unable to tolerate intimacy with his girl friend. In the self-deception, he could identify both with mother's deception of father with respect to her family's poverty, and father's deception in the lawsuit, as well as mockery toward his Bar Mitzvah. The primal scene anxieties occasioned by the movie theater had been augmented by other violent scenes, as the suicide, whose impact he had tried to cope with by denial of the reality of the memory. His fear of the loss of girl friends had prototypes in father's stormy dismissal of nurses. The inference of deep oral fears is based on the prolonged finger sucking, food preoccupations, and especially the merging experience of intercourse. It seemed that the fear of trains not stopping was related not only to the excitement of motion, but also contained the symbolic reverse of the "time has stopped" notion, namely, that his own progress could not be arrested.

Case 5

The patient, a thirty-six-year-old single woman, began analysis four years ago. She had a fear of men and multiple phobias (street, theater, elevator, conveyances) representing a projection and displacement of exhibitionistic, masochistic, scoptophilic and oral-sadistic impulses. As a child, she was passive, compliant, and hesitant, with vague fears of the street and of being alone. Counterphobically, she enjoyed traveling and working abroad for the government. There had been an almost complete absence of sexual interest or experience until several years before the analysis, when she intellectually decided to have sexual relations with men, which she did promiscuously with the help of alcohol. She became increasingly anxious and, six months prior to the analysis, her phobia broke out while watching a play in which a slave was beating a woman. The patient is extremely passive with a severe inhibition of aggression and a tendency to depression which is kept in check by excessive use of alcohol.

Though passive and clinging, she has a good relation with people when at ease. There is no evidence of schizophrenia. She has a great intolerance of psychic pain and uses the mechanisms of avoidance, denial, suppression, and repression extensively. Her analytic material is scattered, vague, and headlined, with much forgetting. There is a strong tendency to act out both within and outside the analysis. There is a certain childishness in her makeup involving primary-process thinking and particularly animism, which is striking in her humor, her way of looking at things, and her symptoms. However, most dramatic are temporary ego disturbances which accompany her severe anxiety attacks to varying degrees.

According to the patient's verbalizations, things (e.g., waiting room) or people (e.g., analyst) seem different or unfamiliar. Things don't seem the same in the sense of being part of a known, familiar organization pattern. She describes them as being "like before you are born or as an infant." She fears confusing stop lights and walking the wrong way ("almost got hit by a car"). She cannot trust her sense of distance or geography, and fears bumping into people or into a lamp post. She is not sure, by walking a block in the right direction, that the place she wants to go to will be there, or that she will get there. She cannot trust judgment or conveyances, be sure a train will go where it is supposed to, or that she will get off at the right place. Her conception of geography is small spots that she knows and the unknown in between. In stores, she cannot focus on or place familiar objects.

Her walk is unsteady, she is afraid of falling, walking is no longer automatic. After an analytic hour, for example, she felt cheerful, without anxiety, but somewhat woozy and had difficulty walking. Her legs would not seem to work properly; she had to concentrate on their functioning as if part of her was observing herself, or someone else's will was moving her legs "like watching a child trying to learn to walk, sympathizing but unable to help."

The patient suffers from varying degrees of amnesia. She cannot keep things straight in her head. She has a feeling that her thoughts do not follow a known pattern, are disorganized, and almost not a part of herself and that she has to concentrate and attend to them. On one occasion, the patient felt that there was no past or future, only the present. During an analytic hour, with little anxiety, she began to feel she was operating at several levels—that she was talking and did not know what she would say next, that it didn't even feel as if she were talking. The room seemed unfamiliar and she had to keep looking around it to assure herself that parts of it were familiar. There was no meaningful context or connection with past or future. The objects in the room loomed large in comparison with the walls. They seemed to get closer and "impended," or hovered over her frighteningly.

At times the patient does not know who she is or who the other person is. She wonders how other people look at things from a different angle or how a dog might feel about things. "How nice to be inside someone else to see how they feel and sense things." She feels that a man differs from a woman only in that he has a penis attached to him and wonders how this feels. She assumes that it is similar to the fact that her feet are attached to her. She has feelings of unreality when she is not sure who the other person is—"it's as if the other person really is no different than a chair." She imagines the chair in the analyst's office has eyes or lurks behind a desk. As she talks this way, she begins to experience a slight feeling of unreality, and wouldn't be surprised if the chair got larger or smaller. It's like *Alice in Wonderland*. When she was a child, her stuffed animals and dolls were real people, whereas grown-ups were not. She feels better with the drapes closed in her apartment, like in the womb. When she felt strange on the street, it was as if she would withdraw into herself and peer out—as if she were inside herself and her body was a conveyance which she could trust no more than she could trust a bus. She has a funny feeling about touching something or being touched while on the street, as if there would be no more sensation than if the wall or her apartment were touched. She does not know how she looks or how her apartment looks. The analyst frequently looks different.

It should be mentioned also that there had been considerable inhibition in eating, helped by alcohol. Objects and people are much more real to the patient if she can touch them rather than just perceive them; although she has seen and touched a penis, she cannot reproduce it in her memory, is completely confused as to how it works, and has never been able to draw this part of a man's anatomy.

The above experiences might be separated into three overlapping categories: (1) instinctualization of certain ego functions along the line of hysterical symptoms and inhibitions (e.g., perception, walking, judgment of distance); (2) depersonalization and estrangement; and (3) partial, temporary regression to earlier ego states or experiences.

Depersonalization and estrangement seem to warrant a separate category. Recently, the patient came to her analytic hour with a "thought stuck in her craw." Several days later it came out that the thought was, "I want your breast." In the interim, she described how she handled disturbing thoughts or the feeling that there might be disturbing thoughts in her head. She both consciously and automatically (and it is hard to separate these) does not look around in her mind for fear of what she will bump into. She equates this with her fear to look to the right or left when she used to be anxious in her apartment—for fear she might see something like a pillar or post, suddenly or unexpectedly. It was not that what she perceived might stir up disturbing thoughts; it was a direct projection of the inner process to the outside. She also likened the inability to look in her thoughts to the inability to look at or place objects in stores. Thus there may be a sequence such as: conscious avoidance—denial and isolation—estrangement—repression. The withdrawal of cathexis from the inner thought (object representation or impulse) seems to be projected onto the outside, resulting in estrangement.

The precipitating situation for the anxiety attacks and the ego disturbances is the stimulation of forbidden impulses, primarily oedipal in nature, and intimately connected with the primal scene. There results an ego regression. In the instance described above when, without manifest anxiety, she could not walk automatically after her analytic hour, she had, during the hour, been doting on the analyst as an omnipotent parent. She regressed to infancy. This was a defense against her oedipal impulses, as was the other instance described when, during the analytic hour, incestuous wishes just acted out with a married man were brought into the transference and she had the feeling that the room was strange, the furniture large and impending, and she had no awareness of the analyst's presence, whereas formerly he had sadistically "impended" on her.

The material suggests that the depersonalization and ego regressions are triggered by the same stimuli that trigger the panic attacks (innumerable situations stirring up forbidden libidinal and aggressive impulses). The panic attacks may be enhanced secondarily by the ego changes. Like a vicious cycle, the panic attack may secondarily enhance the ego regression both by reason of withdrawal of available energy and by regressive attempts at mastery. This cycle was not broken until a more active type of mastery could be utilized by the patient—until one night, while having sexual thoughts, she was able to "tell off" the punitive image of her mother. Gradually, as the analysis progressed, uncontrolled panic became controlled anxiety attacks with little or no ego disturbance.

One can only speculate as to why these phenomena occur in this woman. Generally speaking, there is a great deal of orality (alcohol, dependency, depressive tendencies) and her ego operates in part on primitive levels—primary process, animism, intolerance of pain (pleasure ego), helplessness, inability to assert herself, and failure of active mastery. These factors contribute to the severe anxiety attacks and to the regressive ego phenomena. More specifically, the ego disturbances may also repeat perceptions, body feelings, or ego changes experienced at an early age when witnessing the primal scene, and possibly later repeated with masturbation (for example, confusion of self and nonself, male and female, changes in size, intrauterine fantasies, etc.). The analytic material is replete with references to the primal scene, but it is not recalled. She is constantly struggling with the temptation to masturbate but does not recall ever having done so.

Case 6

A thirty-seven-year-old woman, a former dancer, came for analysis with the complaint of alternating anger and depression, or denials of both.

In one session, the patient complained of the inability to judge distances so that she bumped into people on the street, and was fearful of an automobile accident while driving because of uncertainty as to how far away her car was from another. Several months ago, she was in an actual automobile accident while teaching a friend how to drive; one determinant appears to have been the patient's lack of awareness of their speed (distance ÷ time) which was excessive for a beginner. She stated also, "I can see only two feet ahead of me." In the same session, she felt like a small child with her feet so small that her shoes felt too large and might fall off. She felt as if she were floating and might float away like a balloon. She imagined the analyst as a woman holding and cuddling her.

As for the comment, "I can see only two feet ahead of me," the patient found it distressing to see the analyst's feet in her peripheral vision. To avoid seeing them, she would either turn her whole body diagonally on the couch, or she would turn her head away from his feet. She did the latter with a great deal of muscular tension and, on several occasions, developed a stiff neck.

This session occurred while the patient was sitting up. Five weeks previously she was instructed to sit up because she avoided looking at the analyst and remained unaware of his existence. He was only a "voice" with no personal life. Over weekends, he "crawled into the woodwork." In sitting up, she was, in effect, forced to look at the analyst and at his feet. It is suggested that her difficulty in judging distances is based on a fantasy of a fixed focus at two feet of distance as a defense against seeing the analyst's two feet. This would appear to have occurred on the basis of a primary-process play on the ambiguous meaning of "feet"—as distance and as anatomy. The symptom, inability to judge distances, seems to represent a fixed distance focus at two feet—the substitution of seeing two feet of distance for seeing two anatomical feet. Thus, the wish and the defense are combined in the symptom.

Feet came into the analysis in other ways. At the beginning of the analysis, she "danced" on the couch. She consistently removed her shoes and, behind raised legs, secretly wiggled her feet when angry. Wiggling them in secret and keeping them far from the analyst related to the fantasy of kicking him in the "shins," later the "ass," and later the "testicles." It is noted she married a man with one testicle. She had the compulsion to touch the analyst's penis, with the obsessive doubt as to whether he had one. She was afraid of his feet as being too big and powerful. Analysis was for her a surgery of the mind, and connected with Dr. B., who removed her uterus, and Dr. W., who in childhood told her (erroneously) that she had rheumatic heart disease and should not get married, have sexual relations, or a baby. At age seven, when in bed with two young uncles, who "urinated" on her, she ran to the bathroom and put adhesive tape on her vagina. At age five, she sat on the front porch of her home while mother was inside expecting a baby that day. Her memory is that one of the uncles chopped down a tree in the back yard and she then ran to mother terrified, saying that a frightening red man was coming down the street. Mother said it wasn't so.

There was a great deal of primal scene material—presented mainly in terms of how she manged not to know what was going on. Her idea of the primal scene was sadomasochistic and oral, with father as a "sex maniac." There were numerous fights between mother and father about money. There were several brief separations and, when the patient was fourteen, a final break when father left. At this point the patient felt confused as to her role in relation to the idea of earning money to support the family, with the fantasy of one day earning a great deal of money to provide comfort for mother and sisters. This she has since acted out by way of secretly giving her husband's money to them.

In addition to difficulty in looking at the analyst's feet while sitting up, he at times appeared blurred to her and somehow different. She would rub her eyes or look at him with one eye to see him more clearly. Her blindness was an identification with her father who had retinitis pigmentosa. She had been told recently that as a child she would play "being blind," in imitation of father.

Touching was a problem for the patient. She feared to get too close to the analyst and entered and left the consultation room with a carefully controlled "ritualistic dance" (originally she was a ballet dancer). When she gave her check, she would do so with trembling hand. This was clearly related to the fear and wish to touch the analyst's penis. However, the sense of touch had never been impaired.

The instinctualization of looking, the avoidance of looking, and the emphasis on touching appear to be related to the father's blindness. An important event was the father's touching her breast on the stairway as he reached forward to feel his way. This occurred when she was fourteen and proud of her breasts. It was a pleasurable experience, but she was furious when father told mother.

Case 7

The patient is a young woman who came for analysis because of depression, inability to experience positive feelings, and anorexia with occasional bulimia. After about one year of analysis, she developed a delusion concerning her body. She believed that she was pregnant and had to wear a coat during the session. If the analyst saw her protruding abdomen, he would take her baby away. This delusion was operative during the analytic sessions but did not materially effect her behavior during the rest of the day. These episodes lasted a few days and have occurred five or six times during the analysis.

Gradually, the following circumstances and interpretations developed about the symptom. She would be depressed the night before and would wake up in the middle of the night with a strong craving for food; then she would stuff herself with cookies, cake, and candy. Her mother was aware of this need and kept the cupboard well supplied. The next day, during her hour, she would not remove her coat. At first, she would not want the analyst to see her "bloated belly." Later, she stated that she had a baby inside and did not want it seen. She felt ashamed and smug at such times. Part of her ego recognized this as a delusion and would attempt to remove her coat, but each time there was too much anxiety and she left the coat on.

As the analysis continued, it became evident that this was a substitute for masturbation. She would fantasy that an enormous penis was entering and tearing her apart and, as she approached orgasm, she felt triumphant and thought: "I've got it." When this fantasy became conscious and she masturbated, she usually didn't eat or ate very little and didn't have to wear her coat. When the delusion invaded her ego, she believed she got the baby from the analyst and now she felt complete: "Everyone has a man, now I have a baby."

At various times during the analysis, she expressed her oral fixation in different ways. For example, after one night's eating bout, she stated that she felt as though she were "in a cocoon of Malomars." These chocolate cookies had always been her favorite. On another, similar occasion, she asked the analyst whether she looked like a piece of candy—she had eaten a lot of candy the night before. In one dream, a man was looking into her vagina as in a gynecological examination and said to her, "You are safe, you have 123 pounds up there." This was her body weight. A recently uncovered, important detail of her psychology is that her father bites to show his affection. As a child, when she cried because he bit too hard, he was surprised and hurt— he only meant love.

These episodes occur as part of a depression which, on a few occasions, was associated with a real loss. Once her mother left to visit her sister in another city. On another occasion, the analytic fee had been raised after her "hidden money" had come out in the analysis. It appears she re-experiences the loss of her fantasied penis and brings about a delusional restoration by eating. Symbolically, she has incorporated her father's and the analyst's penis. In the past year or so, in many dreams, she is the analyst.

Another determinant in this symptom is her sadistic wish to tease and exhibit herself. She fantasies that the analyst will go mad with desire for her and both rape her and give her whatever she wants. She will be in control and the analyst out of control. This brought up the enuresis of her childhood. In the latter half of her childhood, there was extensive teasing, sex play, and nudity among her siblings, of whom she was the youngest.

It is hypothesized that the particular distortion of ego may be explained as a disturbance of body image of delusional intensity in which she has a baby, has a penis, and is her mother's phallus.

Case 8

The patient is a thirty-seven-year-old married man who came to analysis with two chief complaints: (1) recent and intermittent potency problems, chiefly a weak erection, and (2) a work inhibition.

The potency disturbance began during an extramarital affair and was attributed to his fear of the relationship being discovered and his growing awareness of his partner's precarious mental health. The work inhibition was illustrated by his inability to get started on writing his doctoral dissertation. The patient had been teaching undergraduates, and had completed his own graduate work except for the thesis. In the four years in graduate school, he had not been able to select a subject, much less begin studying it. He dated his manifest work inhibition from the birth of his first child, at which time his wife had a post-partum psychosis.

The patient's past history revealed that he was the second of three children, having a sister six years older and a sister three years younger. He reported that his mother had died when he was about six years old and he had few memories of her. The father was described as indulgent to babies, but distant and critical of children as they grew older. From early childhood, the patient remembers being embarrassed by his father, who appeared less successful than other fathers, comical or ridiculous, shy, easily embarrassed, and subservient. He contrasted his mother, a schoolteacher, as gentle and affectionate with his father, who was coarse, dirty, and uneducated.

His older sister became the drudge of the household after the mother's death. She had few friends, did all the cooking and serving, nagged and quarreled, and was easily upset and frequently tearful. To his surprise, she married when he was in college, but stayed in her father's house. While the patient was in the Army, she became psychotic and died in a state mental hospital. The patient, during the analysis, reproached himself for not being more active in protecting her from her unhappy family role, and for not seeking more adequate psychiatric care for her during her illness.

The younger sister married shortly after this and lived with her husband in the father's house. She was poor and barely able to manage on her husband's limited salary. She had to care for the father, who was critical of his son-in-law and at times quite suspicious of him. In spite of the patient's good fortune in marrying a rich woman, he did not feel free to help his sister.

At the beginning of treatment, the patient was uncertain of the cause of the mother's death, which at first seemed to be some type of gynecological illness. However, from dream material, a suggestion was made that she had been depressed and had committed suicide. This, after repeated denials by the father, was finally admitted by him to be the truth.

The prolonged and repeated traumas in the patient's life can be seen from the schedule of these events. The mother became pregnant with the third child when the patient was two and a half. Shortly after the birth of his younger sister, she became depressed and, after a year and a half of this illness, she managed to kill herself with rat poison.

The patient recalls a scene in which the father told him the mother was very sick. The patient feels he knew then she was dead but told his father, "Don't cry, Daddy, on such a beautiful and shiny day." This scene had been the prototype of his denial of trouble.

In the patient's psychosexual development, his earliest memory was of being corrected for urinating in the bathtub while being bathed. After his mother's death, he recalls a great hunger for milk with his meals; he would consume over a quart at a time, so that it had to be rationed. He remembers a childhood effort to push his penis into his younger sister's rectum. He was given enemas by his father during latency at the same time as they were administered to his younger sister. At puberty, he shaved his pubic hair in order to conceal the pubertal changes from his father, believing his somewhat precocious sexual development was related to masturbation.

From the point of view of treatment, the main defenses on which the patient has relied have been denial, isolation, and primitive introjective and projective mechanisms. The dominant mood is a stoical resignation with an underlying depression. The patient has been in analysis for five years. Two occasions in the course of the analysis are described below.

The first occurred in the two hours before a summer vacation. Although this was not his first vacation during treatment, it was the most intense reaction to the forthcoming separation. Also, the patient had finally written an article reviewing some books of literary criticism, of which he had been quite critical.

The hour started by his saying he was in a panic that he would be discovered to be "crazy," have made no sense, and therefore be criticized in turn. Next he stated he felt unreal, felt he was going to fall off the couch, that he was standing by the couch and watching himself. Then he became very sleepy and had a series of "dreams" on the couch related to quinces—"the Queen's apples." He heard his wife saying "The Queen's apples are soggy." These images or dreams were followed by a jumbled phrase involving the words "good sleep" or "good night."

In the next hour he reported a horrifying experience of seeing a beggar on the sidewalk who seemed to him not only to have no legs, but literally to have no pelvis. He had just seen *Moby Dick* and had been reading *A Walk on the Wild Side,* in which a very brutal scene takes place between two men, one of whom has no legs and propels himself on skate wheels. He had rewritten his essay in a panic and had had a hallucinationlike dream of turtles snapping at him. He felt he might go crazy and that he needed a tranquilizer. He was aware of a tortured, powerful wish to be close to the therapist, not leave for his vacation, and to do anything to please the therapist. Toward the end of the hour, he had a fantasy of being a German world conqueror—a Hitler-like figure. This was followed by a feeling that he was large and his body was that of a child, a bodily experience similar to those he felt in childhood when feverish.

It was felt in these two hours that the immediate stimulus to his panic was the separation for the summer, combined with the successful completion of his first literary effort. The two meant a denouncement of his father, a quarreling followed by death. This mobilized feelings of unreality and depersonalization. In order to avoid the rivalry or quarrel, the patient regressed to the wish that he had never been separated from his father, which also means he is his mother (the schoolteacher) and will become crazy as she did. The fear of criticizing or being criticized was related to his mother's death, on one level representing the fight between his parents leading to the mother's pregnancy, castration, and death, and on another level the fight between himself and his father over the question of who was guilty for his mother's death—the patient for his fantasied oral or phallic attack, or the father for his phallic attack.

The second episode occurred over a period of three days and was again related to aggressive destructive feelings, this time more clearly directed toward the therapist as a rival. Interestingly, a likely concomitant stimulus to these feelings was a change in the analytic couch. There had been a change from a leather couch to a foam rubber mattress type. On noticing a change, he commented that it was less Viennese as if there had been a new independence. The therapist could follow his own line of thought, the bright new American way of doing things; he felt less at home with more concern about lying down. The old couch was like a barber's chair where he could receive attention passively. He ended on a not unusual note, "None of this sounds like anything but chatter."

Following this, there was no mention of the couch until a week later. During this week's interval the patient's secretary wanted to consult an analyst and he then asked if he could give her the analyst's name. It was in this setting that the patient mentioned his readiness to throw himself into the analyst's arms, using his wife's money. He had to ask his father-in-law for additional funds, and received the check but no letter was enclosed. He added, "I expected him to be pleased," then, "I feel sleepy; I go into a daze." He felt as if he were giving up his arms and legs in order to be carried. He thought of an unnerving fantasy that his secretary went to an analyst to confess she had a penis; he had an image of sticking his head through a boy's legs; he thought of himself as helpless, with no energy. The next day, about half-way through the hour, he again became tired and drowsy. He had a fantasy of his older sister's breasts—he thought of an article on Freud's theory of culture followed by a vision of a red-headed girl with green eyes, a drugstore gold-digging type, an image of a communist worker, angry, or a Hungarian revolutionist, accusing the patient of being a parasite.

In the third hour he started by mentioning a feeling of lurching toward the old couch. He thought of a number of childhood playmates, some of whom had lost their mothers, but had not been as unsuccessful as he. Again he felt sleepy and enjoyed the "useful contact with the unconscious." He felt breathless and hollow. He became aware of his windpipe and lungs. He had a vivid dream image of a toy railroad with toy dolls in wooden houses. He saw tiny models of Christmas trees. The toys were standing on discs made of cork. He saw water spilling from a faucet in a sink with a white enamel pot in it. It flowed over. He thought of the Christmas trees—one had fallen to the ground and was half-eaten, a sodden cakelike tree. He felt breathless, empty, sleepy. He thought of being given an enema and feeling empty.

In summary, one can see the situation of possible rivalry and jealousy which the patient could experience in the triangular situation of the therapist, patient, and patient's secretary. The images progress from the wish to be the father's dependent, to be carried, ending with a wish to be the father's phallus. In the second hour there seemed to be a memory of his anger and rivalry with his younger sister, and the wish that he could be the parasite at the breast. In the third hour, there was some reference to a respiratory incorporation, next a possible memory of being scolded for urinating in the bathtub, combined with a feeling of crying for his dead mother and ending in a compromise breast-phallus image, the sodden cakelike tree.

In each hour the interpretation was made that the sleepy, dazed state was a regressive defense against aggressive and rivalrous feelings against the therapist, with the genetic background being his oedipal problem—the father killing the mother and forbidding the patient any phallic masculinity. His castration wish was related to his own fear of his mother's vulnerability, and his fear that rivalry with his father would end in his or in his father's death. Finally, the oedipal rivalry was regressively represented as separation anxiety or an experiencing of the warded-off depression which followed his mother's death. The depression was experienced as a reunion with the dead mother.

Alternate to these interpretations are Lewin's (1954, 1955) formulations. The patient's behavior on the couch represents a wish to sleep in preference to facing the rivalry and separation from the father; the couch represents the mother's body. The manifest content of the dream as given in the associations and the latent content is a merging with the father-analyst and an earlier preoedipal merging with the phallic mother.

A difficult and specific defense has been that the content of the analyst's interpretations has been ignored and dealt with either as a lullaby tending to prolong the happy dream, or as an intruding, scolding voice tending to waken. This is described by Lewin.

The report is given to illustrate two points: (1) In the two examples presented the ego regression follows a libidinal wish. (2) The command on the father's part to forget the mother's illness and suicide shows parallels to Rosen's (1955) case. The apparent effect of this on the patient has been to interpret it as an order not to think or trust his own judgment. Conversely, any comments of the therapist should be agreed to, but are untrue. This has been a very difficult resistance. His compliance, which has marked the analysis, also seems to stem from an effort to make up to his mother for not following her example and killing himself.

Discussion

Prior to a discussion of the clinical material, it should be emphasized once again that the phenomena under consideration consist of transitory occurrences involving various ego functions, as they were noted in the course of an ongoing analysis. Much of the clinical material submitted suggested more permanent or long-range distortion of such ego functions as object relationships, thought processes, the synthetic function, etc. These aspects of the material, however, were not the main focus of the discussion, which was rather on the transitory disturbance of an autonomous function appearing during the analysis. In this sense, it was striking that of the eight clinical examples presented to the group for consideration, five involved some distortion of the body image, four disturbances of perception were noted, reality testing was directly affected in three of the examples, the sense of time and of distance judging were involved in two cases, and phenomena of depersonalization appeared in two situations. Two other instances dealt with either the Isakower phenomenon or drowsiness on the couch. These are not the usual disturbances of ego functions reported in the psychoanalytic literature. By and large, the emphasis has been upon long-standing disturbances, while those of a more transitory nature have not been reported. Also noteworthy from a phenomenologic point of view, was the fact that there might be more than one specific ego function involved in the clinical material reported. For example, in Case 3, the disturbances involved the body image, self-representation, perception, and reality testing simultaneously. In contrast, Case 4 had specific involvement of the time sense only.

The contrast between these two cases points up a clinical impression gained from the various cases presented. The occurrence of ego distortions and the involvement of one or more autonomous functions in such distortions seems related to the capacity of the given ego to deal with all conflictual situations. The greater the resiliency of the ego to adapt or erect defenses without regression, the less is the involvement of autonomous functions in conflict. The converse also seems true.

In all of the clinical situations described, the precipitating cause of the regression is the presence of anxiety and the need of the ego to deal with an anxiety-provoking situation. Most frequently, the anxiety arose in situations or under conditions which stimulated an id wish, either libidinal or aggressive in nature. In only one instance (Case 3) is the contribution of a superego command to anxiety production specifically clear in the material given. The nature of the anxiety produced by the id wish and/or superego command seems most often to be associated with castration anxiety, but it is clear from the clinical cases studied that no one type of anxiety is involved exclusively in initiating the ego regressions described. Separation anxiety is evident in the material. It is especially worthy of note that primal-scene experiences are frequent in the data and often seem to be connected with the anxiety-provoking situation. The latter observation is probably connected with the castration anxiety that is frequently seen as the initiating force for the particular regression.

It is evident that, in each instance, the ego regression served a defensive function in relation to the situation in which it occurred, but the nature of the defense varied. For example, while regression serves a denying function in several instances (Case 1, Case 2, Case 4), it is also clear that the distortion of time sense serves as a vehicle for doubting the validity of certain early life experiences (Case 4). This element of uncertainty is present also in Case 5, and in both of these cases this additional aspect is defensive in nature. Perusal of the clinical material shows, however, that the regressive phenomena serve more than a defensive role. It is evident, for example, from the material of Case 6, that the regressive phenomenon present (distortion of distance judgment) is associated with a fantasy having to do with feet in both the linear and anatomical sense. This example indicates not only the distortion of distance judgment, but also an involvement of the process of thinking in the regressive phenomena, so that a more primitive type of thinking, characterized by symbolization and displacement, is manifest (these are aspects of what is usually referred to as primary-process thinking). Thus the regressive phenomena provide a discharge for certain parts of a fantasy involving feet. In Case 3, the regressive phenomena associated with disturbance of the body image are connected with and provide a discharge for certain unconscious feminine wishes. The regressive phenomena represent not only defensive maneuvers against a current anxiety situation, but also seem to represent the discharge of certain unconscious wishes of a libidinal or aggressive nature. The net conclusion from this aspect of the clinical material is that the distortions of an ego function arise in reaction to the existence of some anxiety situation, but are also utilized by the ego to discharge certain unconscious wishes which may come from id, ego, or superego. Thus these phenomena are multidetermined and follow the law of multiple function as described by Waelder (1936). In this regard, Case 7 demonstrates the multiple function of the regressive phenomena, since the bodily delusion presented by the patient fulfills and provides gratification for wishes arising from the oedipal level of development as well as manifestations belonging to the phallic and oral periods. Involved in the regressive phenomena in this example are fantasies of having a baby, being a phallus, and of having the breast, as well as the sadistic wish to tease.

Consideration of the nature of the economics involved in the regressive phenomena under discussion led first to a review of the concept of the gradual neutralization of instinctual energies as the ego and its specific functions mature (Hartmann, 1958). Primitive libidinal and aggressive instinctual forces carry the stamp of their origin and nature and press for immediate discharge along appropriate channels. As the ego functions cathected with these energies develop, there is also a change in the instinctual forces in the direction of becoming neutralized, i.e., losing their original libidinal and/or aggressive nature, and also the pressure for immediate discharge. A fully autonomous ego function utilizes fully neutralized energy. When such a function regresses or becomes involved in conflict, it becomes suffused with less neutralized energies or, conversely, it becomes suffused with more sexualized or aggressified instinctual energy. This may come about either through a loss of neutralization, i.e., the neutral energy becomes reinstinctualized (either relibidinized or reaggressified), or through an influx of unneutralized energy, or through a combination of both. It would appear that the greater the regression of the ego function, the greater is the degree of reinstinctualization of the energies involved.

Examining the material more closely, it is possible to see that, involved in almost all of the examples, is an aspect of ego functioning which is very familiar to analysts in their clinical practice, that of the interrelationship which exists among various ego functions. Although the examples represent distortions of specific ego functions which have achieved autonomy, it is evident throughout much of the material that other ego functions are involved to some extent. This is particularly true in terms of the function of object relationships in that some of the background necessary for the occurrence of the phenomena under discussion involves the nature of the object relationships of the patient. In Case 6, identification with the blind father contributes to the reinstinctualization of the function of looking, the avoidance of looking, and an emphasis on touching. In Case 5, the necessary background for the distortion of time sense has to do with an effort to deny seeing a suicide when the patient was seven or eight. His father's urging him to lie in certain situations reinforced his utilization of this particular defense. This denial of reality associated with the father played a part in his ability to deny the reality of the passage of time in the present situation.

In Case 2, the distortion of object relations involves a set of foster parents: a weak, alcoholic father, and a mother who allowed the foster parent situation to exist and aided and abetted its occurrence. The Isakower phenomenon that Case 2 showed represented, among many other things, a hostility to her unborn child (she was pregnant at the time), as well as what may have been fantasies associated with the early months of her life, in which the patient had been given a very dilute formula on which she gained little or no weight and which led to a state of chronic dissatisfaction. The importance of the early relationships with objects is particularly evident in this case and, in fact, this particular clinical example raises another question which has been touched upon in the discussion of Case 5.

It is felt that, for Case 5, there might be another explanation than that of regression of an ego function and/or reinstinctualization of the energies involved. A possibility touched upon for this case, as well as for Case 2, has to do with the partial reactivation of earlier ego states or experiences. In Case 5, these would be perceptions, body feelings, or ego changes experienced at an early age when witnessing the primal scene, and probably repeated later with masturbation. The patient was constantly giving material replete with references to the primal scene, but the actual memory of the event was not recalled. It is questioned whether the various regressive manifestations described for Case 5 represent the memory of certain ego states. In Case 2, where the Isakower phenomenon occurs, this possibility also exists, that is, a re-enactment of the bodily and physical sensations associated with very early ego experiences.

The considerations stated above stimulated one of the most intense discussions in the Group as to the possibility of differentiating between reinstinctualization of certain ego functions and actual states of regression of ego functions to more primitive stages of the development of the particular function concerned. Strictly speaking, regression implies return to an earlier, less specialized type of functioning or a less specialized structure. The classic example might be used of differentiating between so-called secondary-process thinking which is not only reality-directed and logical, but also utilizes neutralized energy, in contrast to the so-called primary-process thinking, which is directed toward immediate discharge utilizing non-neutralized energy and is characterized by certain modes of functioning, such as displacement and symbolization, which are nonlogical. Although in earlier psychoanalytic writing it is regarded as regressive for primitive thinking to appear in the course of an analysis, it has come to be recognized that, in fact, the primary-process mode of functioning is omnipresent and is overlaid by the more advanced form of energy discharge. Thus the manifestations of the earlier modes of thinking can be seen frequently in very normal situations, for example in wit, humor, and in the many parapraxes of everyday life. From this point of view, the transitory regressive phenomena described can be regarded as normal phenomena, particularly the example of the Isakower phenomenon, which can be regarded as a normal concomitant of falling asleep. In addition, such factors as illness or fatigue at various times of the day, particularly toward the end of the day, may lend strength to the appearance of the phenomena under discussion.

But the question remains, how to differentiate such occurrences, which are relatively normal and do not represent regression in the literal sense of a return to a developmentally earlier form of structure or function, but rather, represent the reappearance of modes of functioning which are omnipresent in the ego and which are merely overlaid by the later, more advanced forms of the development of the various ego functions.

Another question that was raised in this context was whether the clinical examples cited could not be regarded as conversion symptoms, since there was often a symbolic meaning to the ego distortion present, e.g., Case 6. The answers that emerged from this discussion had to do with the nature of the precipitating cause (the anxiety-provoking situation), the transience of the manifestation, the involvement of a usually autonomous ego function in the service of a defense or adaptation to a conflict, and finally the utilization of less neutralized energies as manifested by increased pressure of discharge phenomena. The observation that many of the clinical examples given provided for gratification of a fantasy (e.g., in Case 3, of a fantasy of being feminine) does not make it the same as a conversion symptom as seen in hysteria. In the latter condition, aside from other considerations, the conversion manifestation does not usually involve an autonomous ego function. Most particularly, the conversion manifestation depicts both wish and defense simultaneously with the overt manifestation being a compromise product.

It was questioned whether there might be a still different way of regarding the ego distortions under consideration. So far in the discussion, ego functions had been presented as being subject to either simple regression, i.e., a return to a more primitive state, structure, or function, or to reinstinctualization of the function through its involvement in a specific conflict situation. It was felt that consideration should be given to the possibility that there could be arrests in the development of the particular ego function which would, to a degree, correspond to instinctual fixation in the sphere of instinctual development. Following this thought, what would be seen clinically would be a malfunctioning ego activity, such as a poorly developed sense of time or sense of distance judgment, but one that is consistently faulty or defective in its functioning. It is also conceivable that there could be an arrest in development of an ego function followed by maturation, but with a greater susceptibility of the function to regress to the "fixation point" at which such a developmental defect occurred. This concept brought up the question of whether there might not be still another approach to account for the phenomena under consideration.

It was suggested that regression, reinstinctualization, and arrests in development may not cover all possibilities. Perhaps an ego distortion represents a new manifestation, not a new function. It may be the result of hypertrophy of one or more ego functions which produces an aberration that is outside the sphere of normal development. As an analogy, the formation of scar tissue as the normal bodily response to an injury was cited. In some individuals this normal process hypertrophies and a keloid results. This is outside the usual response to an injury and represents pathology. Returning to the psychological sphere, mention was made of those individuals studied by Greenacre (1952) in whom very early, continuous trauma led to accentuation of certain ego functions. The following clinical example was outlined briefly, in which an ego function (aesthetic contemplation) was involved in what was regarded as an overflow manifestation resulting from this patient's very peculiar relationship with her mother.

A young woman in her early years was constantly under the supervision of her mother in eating and defecating. The mother would chew with her when she was chewing and she had to swallow when the mother said, "Swallow." The mother would also watch her bowel movements and grunt along with her as if she were forcing the stool simultaneously out of her body and the daughter's. This patient, later in life, developed a disturbance in looking at certain, rather violent modern paintings. She had a fear that if she became absorbed in a painting, something dreadful would happen. The ego function involved here was aesthetic contemplation. To become absorbed in a painting was like becoming absorbed in mother, and she could be emptied out entirely.

The essence of the discussion which followed was that a different and useful way of looking at the same phenomena had been suggested, but that the clinical example was not conclusive. Many of the discussants felt that what was described was essentially a reinstinctualization of a usually autonomous ego function. It was felt that the best understanding of such phenomena possible at this point in our knowledge, is in terms of a reinstinctualization by libidinal and/or aggressive energy of an ego function which has developed to the stage of secondary autonomy. This view supposes that in the course of development there occurs not only a maturation of the function itself, but also a change in the nature of the energies utilized to maintain the function, a change from instinctual to neutralized energy. In the situations under consideration there was a later change in the direction of deneutralization and the utilization of more instinctualized energy. It was felt that the latter change is best understood as a regression to an earlier state of both function and structure, with the utilization of earlier types of energies to carry out this function.

At this stage of the discussion, the point was made that, in all of the clinical examples presented by the members of the panel, in which regression of an ego function occurred, an important aspect of the situation as it occurs clinically had not been considered. In each of these situations the affective response to the particular precipitating occurrence and the isolation of this affective response from the mainstream of mental life were important factors in the ego regression which followed. The regression was in the service of reinforcing the isolation of the affective response to the provoking situation. It was suggested that the nature of the object relationships and of early traumata in the relationship between the child and parent prior to the age of eighteen months play a part in determining the fragility of the ego in patients in whom such regressions occur.

It was stressed further that not only the role of the parents, but also the relationship to other siblings and the precise nature of the transference in the analysis on the occasion in which the regression occurs, all play an important role in reviving the anxiety situations which lead to the regression—a regression which, in turn, partially repeats the earlier relationship to the object.

An attempt was made to outline a conceptual framework for the type of partial ego regression under discussion, based on the clinical impression that the patients reported had "weakened" egos. A scale, ranging from severe pathology at one extreme, to health at the other, was proposed for consideration as a useful tool in evaluating manifestations of ego regression. At the severe pathology end would be phenomena seen in the most regressed psychoses. Ego regression at the healthy end of the scale would include those phenomena seen in artistic productions or in free associations (regression in the service of the ego [Kris, 1952]). The ego regression phenomena under consideration lie between these two extremes, since these phenomena show a regression greater than healthy, yet not so severe as to warrant a diagnosis of psychosis. For example the woman who reported visions when asked to free-associate had regressed further than one might expect of healthy individuals, and yet she was not hallucinating. It was further suggested that etiological factors responsible for the phenomena under discussion range from ninety-nine per cent heredity and one per cent environment, to one per cent heredity and ninety-nine per cent environment. Environmental influences include trauma and object relations. Examples cited were the role of trauma in Case 1 and the role of identifications in Cases 4 and 6. Heredity and/or environment could affect multiple or single ego functions. In individuals showing multiple ego regressions, one would expect a more massive predisposition and/or more massive trauma. With multiple ego regressions, one would also expect a higher incidence of trauma early in life. Conversely, in individuals with single ego regressions, one would expect less severe predispositions and/or less severe and later trauma. It was considered possible that these ego regressions only occur where there is general ego impairment. In other words, ego regression of this type would not occur in a less severe neurotic. The impression gained from the cases presented supports this possibility. Diagnostically, they range from the severe neuroses, through borderline, to mild psychoses. The patients seem to use primitive defense mechanisms such as denial, projection, and introjection more often than usual; somatization and acting out seem more common too. All these aspects suggest that, in general, these patients will need longer than average analyses. In the cases presented, there also seems to be a higher incidence of trauma from realistic experiences. This likewise suggests longer analyses with more working through of the realistic experience than is true for the usual neurotic individual.

Regarding the question of therapy, the members of the panel all agreed that, first of all, each of these phenomena must be analyzed in and of itself like any other analytic material. Only in this way is it possible to understand the nature of the processes described in the clinical case reports. It was also suggested that an additional aspect of working with patients in whom there is extensive impairment of ego functions, is in the nature of establishing a solid relationship between the analyst and patient in the direction of the patient identifying with the analyst, so that the observing part of his ego can be strengthened and can co-operate with the analyst's ego in the work of the analysis (Stewart, 1960, 1963). As to the specific techniques available in such a procedure, many pointed to papers by Leo Stone (1954) who discussed the widening scope of analysis, and Phyllis Greenacre's extensive reports (1952) on treatment of the more severe pregenital character neuroses.

Conclusions

1. Ego regressions (a) have a describable defensive function; (b) can serve as a vehicle for fulfillment of id wishes; (c) can serve as a vehicle for fulfillment of superego demands; (d) generally serve multiple functions, since id, ego, and superego elements may participate in or find discharge through such distortions.

2. In general, the degree of ego distortion appearing during an analysis seems to parallel the severity of the instinctual regression.

3. No specific danger situation is the exclusive anxiety-provoking force to initiate ego regression. Castration anxiety was most frequently encountered in the clinical examples given, but separation anxiety and fear of superego were observed. Primal scene experiences seem to play an especially important role.

4. With respect to genetic factors in ego development predisposing to regression of autonomous ego functions, it was felt that object relations, especially in the earliest phases of life, are of special importance. In certain instances, identification with love objects who themselves showed disturbance of discrete ego functions seemed to facilitate the tendency to regression.

5. The selective regression of various ego functions was emphasized. This was particularly striking in certain areas where selective regression occurred in one of several functionally related activities of the ego. Ego functions relating to perception, reality testing, and the body image seemed most prone to involvement in regressive phenomena.

6. Most often the specific defensive aspect of the regression consisted of a form of denial reinforced by the regression itself.

7. It seemed possible that the regressive phenomena represented a repetition of previous ego states or physical experiences, in the nature of perceptions or bodily feelings.

8. It was felt that the collection of such clinical data as reported here further reinforces the definition of the ego in terms of its functions, each of which has its own developmental and maturational history which can, in principle, be traced out in detail.

BIBLIOGRAPHY

Freud, S. (1923), The Ego and the Id. *Standard Edition*, 19:3-66. London: Hogarth Press, 1961.

Greenacre, P. (1941), The Predisposition to Anxiety. *Psychoanal. Quart.*, 10:66-95, 610-638.

————— (1952), *Trauma, Growth and Personality*. New York: Norton.

Hartmann, H. (1950), Comments on the Psychoanalytic Theory of the Ego. *The Psychoanalytic Study of the Child*, 5:74-96. New York: International Universities Press.

————— (1958), *Ego Psychology and the Problem of Adaptation*. New York: International Universities Press.

—————, Kris, E., and Loewenstein, R. M. (1949), Notes on the Theory of Aggression. *The Psychoanalytic Study of the Child*, 3/4:9-36. New York: International Universities Press.

Isakower, O. (1938), A Contribution to the Psychopathology of Phenomena Associated with Falling Asleep. *Int. J. Psychoanal.*, 19:331-345.

Kris, E. (1952), *Psychoanalytic Explorations in Art*. New York: International Universities Press.

Lewin, B. D. (1954), Sleep, Narcissistic Neurosis and the Analytic Situation. *Psychoanal. Quart.*, 23:487-510.

————— (1955), Dream Psychology and the Analytic Situation. *Psychoanal. Quart.*, 24:169-199.

Rosen, V. (1955), The Reconstruction of a Traumatic Childhood Event in a Case of Derealization. *J. Amer. Psychoanal. Assn.*, 3:211-221.

Stewart, W. A. (1960), The Development of the Therapeutic Alliance in Borderline Patients. Unpublished paper presented to the New York Psychoanalytic Society on October 11, 1960. Abstracted in *Psychoanal. Quart.*, 30:165-167, 1961.*

———— (1963), An Inquiry into the Concept of Working Through. *J. Amer. Psychoanal. Assn.*, 11:474-499.*

Stone, L. (1954), The Widening Scope of Indications for Psychoanalysis. *J. Amer. Psychoanal. Assn.*, 2:567-594.

Waelder, R. (1936), The Principle of Multiple Function. *Psychoanal. Quart.*, 5:45-62.

*This contribution was made after the panel held its meetings.